Ghost Hunting From A to Z

A Scientific Approach to Paranormal Investigation

Lowell J. Lindeman Jr.
James J. Kroenig

The Supernatural Research Group
Reading, Pennsylvania, USA
www.tsrg.org

Ghost Hunting from A to Z
A Scientific Approach to Paranormal Investigation
Copyright © 2010 by Lowell J. Lindeman and James J. Kroenig

Editor:
    Heather Lindeman

Contributing Editors:
    Karen Kroenig
    Kathleen Iglar

ISBN-10   0-9829394-0-X
ISBN-13   978-0-9829394-0-6

First Publication Date August 20, 2010

Published by:
    Pareidolia Publishing
    Reading Pennsylvania, USA

Printed and bound in the United States of America.

Table of Contents

Dedication

As a small child growing up in southern Virginia, I can remember staying up late every Friday night to watch "Dr. Mad Blood", a weekly show that was hosted by a zany character who played B and C horror movies. I can remember asking my parents "Do ghosts and monsters really exist?" to which they emphatically replied "No, they only exist in movies." Little did I know then just how much of an impact that question I asked as a child would have on my life as an adult.

When we started The Supernatural Research Group, we really had no idea how much of our personal time the group would require from each of us. As a result our families have had to endure the burden of our absence due to investigations, promotions and research.

We would like to dedicate this book to our families, more specifically our wives. The support and understanding of our wives and children have made it possible for us to pursue a dream that we have mutually shared since childhood. Without their continued patience and understanding we would never have had the opportunity to learn, grow or experience many of the life altering events that we have had over the years. The entire process has opened our eyes and solidified our faith in God.

It is for this reason that we would like to dedicate this book to them.

Lowell Lindeman, Founder
The Supernatural Research Group
8·20·2010

Preface

Regardless of the driving force compelling you to get involved in or start your own paranormal research team, there are many things that one should know before blindly jumping into the paranormal field. Based on the experience we gained from starting our own paranormal research team we tried to design this book to give you a very solid understanding of what is involved in scientific-based paranormal research. Whether you are a seasoned investigator or just starting out, we think you will find this material of value. Much of the content of this book stems from our efforts to develop training materials for our paranormal group's new members. This is the basic information that we strive to provide to new members, as well as what we have learned along the way from conducting investigations, managing, and promoting our paranormal team. We hope that the information we are providing is of value and helps each and every one of you during your quest to find the truth. You are always welcome to stop by our web site at www.tsrg.org and tell us what you think.

Introduction

You are probably looking at this book and wondering to yourself why someone took the time to write yet another book about ghost hunting. Well, the simple truth is we felt that none of the books currently available do a good job addressing the subject matter from a scientific approach.

This book was written with that in mind. While we do take the time to touch on many of the popular theories out there related to the paranormal, we focus specifically on how to conduct paranormal research utilizing the scientific method. The approach we take to deliver the information contained in this book is unique. We start at the very beginning by talking about the origins of the supernatural and how it has influenced many societies the world over. We use a systematic approach to guide you through all of the information so you have a better chance of understanding the scientific method and are able to apply what you learn to your research.

In addition, we also provide you with information that will allow you to make a better decision regarding how to delve in to paranormal research as well as how deeply you want to get involved. We provide you with information on starting your own group, developing and promoting a website, as well a list of vendors who cater to individuals conducting research of this nature.

Our ultimate goal was to produce a resource that would provide useful information to anyone interested in the supernatural or conducting paranormal research. We hope that we have accomplished this and that you find this publication both useful and informative.

1

MAKING SENSE OF IT ALL

At one time paranormal research was considered taboo and scoffed at by most, especially the scientific community. While the scientific community stands fast by their claims that there is no scientific data to support paranormal belief, it isn't the case anymore as far as society is concerned given the huge success of all the TV shows that are aired each week on networks such as SyFy, A&E and The Discovery Channel. An article published by the Associated Press in early 2008 states that the increase in popularity of the paranormal realm is closely attributed to the great success of television shows, the internet, and the increase in availability of high-tech equipment on the market today which are all geared toward the paranormal field. Although there are skeptics that maintain that "ghost hunting" is nothing more than superstition or a waste of time, there are those who continue to "search" for answers in an attempt to shed some light on the supernatural realm. Regardless of the driving force compelling you to join or start your own paranormal research team, there are many things that one needs to know before blindly jumping into the paranormal research field.

The Supernatural Realm

Whether you realize it or not, the supernatural realm shapes and influences our lives in some form or fashion on a daily basis and has had an influential impact on the formation of many great nations.

The term supernatural is derived from the Latin root super or supra meaning "above", plus natura or nature and is used to define anything that is deemed above or beyond nature. The supernatural realm is literally comprised of all things that mankind has no explanation for. Religion, magic, mythology, and even the paranormal are all considered part of the supernatural realm.

The term supernatural is defined by Merriam-Webster as follows:

"**Supernatural** - of or relating to an order of existence beyond the visible observable universe; especially: of or relating to God or a god, demigod, spirit, or devil"

Main Entry:	su·per·nat·u·ral
Function:	*adjective*
Etymology:	Middle English, from Medieval Latin *supernaturalis,* from Latin *super-* + *natura* nature.
Date of origin:	15th century

Mankind's obsession with the supernatural has existed in some form or fashion since the beginning of time; all one has to do to realize this is look at history or some of the ancient ruins that still remain today. Stonehenge for example, located in southern England on the Salisbury Plains, has been the center of countless tales and theories and dates back to around 2600 BC. Another example is the Nazca Lines, a series of geometric shapes or geoglyphs located in the Nazca Desert of Peru. These formations are only visible from the sky and are alleged to have been constructed by supernatural forces or possibly with the assistance of aliens sometime around 400 and 650 AD.

The examples are endless, as is the speculation which is associated with the countless tales that have been recorded and handed down over the last two millennia. But to truly understand what the term encompasses you need to have a firm grasp on the many different parts that make up the whole.

The supernatural realm is comprised of anything and everything that eludes mankind's ability to either logically explain or comprehend. While our knowledge of the unknown has abated with advances in science and mathematics, the realm of the supernatural is far from being solved. The realm of the supernatural is so immense that the majority of its subtopics can be classified into one of four major categories; Religion, Mythology, Magic and the Paranormal.

Religion – Encompasses all things relating to a higher order, such as God and satan, Angels and demons, Heaven and Hell as well as the human soul.

Mythology – Refers to either the study of myths or a body of myths and can encompass such things as Leprechauns, Elves, Vampires, Astrology and even Greek folklore.

Magic – Encompasses all things related to a means to magically affect the world through various spells, rituals or desires in either

3

a harmful or benevolent way. Magic is believed to embody witchcraft, voodoo, alchemy and divination.

Paranormal – Refers to anything that falls outside the range of normal or scientific explanation. The paranormal realm is vast and includes such things as ghosts or spirits, UFO's, aliens, cryptozoology, psychics, parapsychology and precognition.

Figure 1.1

These four categories are by no means all inclusive and many will argue they are closely related to one another. A good example of this is the relationship that many individuals feel exists between religion and the paranormal realm; more specifically Heaven and Hell, Angels and demons and the eternal struggle between good and evil for the human soul.

4

The Paranormal Realm

While it is important to have a solid understanding of the subject as a whole, this book is dedicated to the paranormal realm and as such we will focus our attention on the many areas of study that comprise the field of study.

The paranormal realm, like the supernatural, includes many different areas of focus. As with the supernatural realm, these areas often overlap. It is important to understand that mainstream science considers the study of anything related to the paranormal anecdotal at best. Given the nature of the subject matter, it is almost impossible to apply proven scientific methods to the field as the phenomenon being studied is inconsistent and unpredictable. That is not to suggest that those of us in the paranormal field should not attempt to apply proven methods while conducting our research.

The areas of focus that are generally agreed upon regarding the paranormal realm are as follows:

- Ghosts and other spiritual entities
- Parapsychology
- Cryptozoology
- Psychic Phenomena
- UFO / Alien Phenomena

In an effort to provide you with a better understanding of the subject matter we are going to discuss each area listed above in more detail.

Ghosts and Other Spiritual Entities

At one time it was a widely held theory in the paranormal field that a ghost or spirit is the soul of a deceased person. This theory has been expanded over the last few decades to include demons and elementals as a result of increased popularity and advances in technology related to paranormal research. Paranormal researchers, or "Ghost Hunters" if you will, are looking to document the existence of life after death using technology to either record images or audio of the deceased.

Parapsychology

Parapsychology is the discipline of study related to psychic phenomena using the scientific method. Researchers in this field are looking for scientific proof of the existence of the following abilities in humans and animals:

> *Telepathy* – The ability to transfer information, thoughts, or feelings via the mind.

> *Precognition* – The ability to "see" future events before they occur.

> *Psychokinesis* – The ability to manipulate time, matter, space, or energy with the mind.

> *Clairvoyance* – The ability to pick up on information about a person or place by focusing ones thought. This ability is often used during Ghost Hunting in an attempt to communicate with the spirits of the departed.
>
> (This list should not be considered all inclusive)

MAKING SENSE OF IT ALL

Cryptozoology

Cryptozoology refers to the study of animals that are considered non-existent to mainstream biology. Researchers involved in this field are actively searching for verifiable proof of the existence of creatures such as Bigfoot, the Yeti, the Loch Ness Monster and the Jersey Devil. Figure 1.2 illustrates some of the better known creatures that fall under the cryptozoology category:

List of well known Cryptides

Name	Description	Reported Location
Beast of Bladenboro	Blood-sucking feline-like predator	North Carolina
Bessie	Lake animal	Lake Erie, North America
Bigfoot	Hominid or primate	North America
Champ	Lake animal	Lake Champlain, North America
Chessie	Sea animal	Chesapeake Bay
Chupacabra	Cross between Reptile and Mammal	Mexico/Puerto Rico
Goatman	Bipedal creature	Wisconsin, Maryland, and New York
Grassman	Bigfoot-like; bipedal creature	Kenmore, Akron, Ohio
The Grinning Man	Extraterrestrial	New Jersey, West Virginia
Jersey Devil	Winged bipedal horse	New Jersey
Loch Ness Monster	Lake animal	Loch Ness, Scotland
Merpeople	Human-Fish	The Seven Oceans and several seas
Mothman	Winged bipedal creature	West Virginia
Ogopogo	Lake animal	Lake Okanagan, Canada
Skunk Ape	Bigfoot-like; bipedal creature	Florida
Thunderbird	Giant bird	North America
Yardly Yeti	Canine like quadraped	Texas, East Coast United States
Yeti	Bigfoot-like; bipedal creature	Himalayas (Asia)
Yowie	Bigfoot-like; bipedal creature	Australia

Figure 1.2

7

UFO / Alien Phenomena

This area of the paranormal realm is dedicated to the study of unidentified flying objects and the possible existence of alien life forms that are reported to have visited our planet. While the area of study has generated great controversy and even greater conspiracy theories, one must remember to keep an open mind to the possibility that intelligent life does exist outside our universe given the vast expanse of the cosmos.

Summary

In this chapter we briefly discussed the supernatural realm and how the paranormal realm relates to it. We looked at some of the areas of study that comprise the paranormal field. In the coming chapters we will delve deeper into the paranormal realm as it relates to ghost hunting, and more specifically the common theories, methods, tools, skills and types of evidence that all paranormal researchers are looking for.

2

PARANORMAL THEORIES

In this chapter we will discuss some of the more common theories that most individuals involved in this field focus on while conducting their investigations. Included will be the types of spirits that one may encounter as well as the theories related to the types of activity that may be recorded. We will also talk about the theories related to how ghosts or spirits possibly affect our environment and the methods currently used to record those changes.

Before we jump into listing the theories it is important to understand that the intent of this chapter is to make you aware of the current theories that exist in the field as well as a general understanding of those theories. To be honest, there is enough information available related to each of these theories to produce several thesis papers on each subject.

Scientific Theory vs. Paranormal Theory

Scientific theory and paranormal theory are two very distinct and different things. Scientific theories are based on reliable observations that result in testable predictions and then explain how those predictions are produced, whereas paranormal theories are based on observations and assumptions while the evidence is either nonexistent or highly contested. A good example of this is the theory related to entities producing an EMF field when they are present. In order for this theory to have merit in the scientific community the EMF fields produced would have to be of a specific frequency and duration which has not been shown to be the case. We would need to be able to prove that in fact an entity was present each time these readings were recorded. The real problem with this is ghosts are extremely unpredictable and do not appear on command.

Did You Know? | *EMF is an abbreviation for the term electromagnetic field. The term refers to a physical field produced by electrically charged objects.*

This is not to suggest that we as paranormal researchers should become discouraged and not employ the scientific method during our investigations. It simply means that those of us in the paranormal field need to work together in order to standardize our research and reporting methods.

Types of Entities

There are more theories than one would care to count related to the possible types of entities that one may encounter during an investigation. We are going to narrow our discussion to the primary types and steer clear of discussing any theories that speculate about the entity's origin, classification, or purpose. Again, it is important to understand that at this time we have no real way to validate any of these theories because we lack the ability to converse in detail directly with entities as well as reproduce our findings at will.

Human Entities

Depending on one's belief system, human entities are believed to be the soul/spirit/energy of someone who at one time walked the face of this planet as a living, breathing human being. It is also believed that these entities can appear in many different forms such as mists, shadow figures, orbs of light or full blown apparitions. It is thought that entities of this nature personify many of the same personality traits that we observe among the living. This implies that one may encounter entities that are helpful, mischievous, angry, sad, or even harmful and threatening.

Human entities are believed to "haunt" a location in one of two ways. The first type is called an "active haunting" which refers to the entity's ability to interact with the living. Characteristics of this type of activity range from direct responses to questions asked during an EVP session, to being touched, pushed or even scratched when provoked.

Did You Know? *EVP is an acronym for the term Electronic Voice Phenomena. The term refers to disembodied voices or sounds captured on an audio recorder during a paranormal investigation.*

The second type is called a "passive haunting" which means that the activity witnessed is nothing more than an event from the past being played over and over again. This theory suggests that energy emitted from the living at times of great stress or trauma can be absorbed and stored by inanimate objects and then played back over and over during the right conditions, producing a scene from the past. The activity witnessed does not interact with the living and show no signs of acknowledgment to those who witness it. Examples of this type of activity can include foot steps, knocking, unexplainable talking or screams, slamming doors or apparitions appearing and walking off through walls. Often the only way to actually discern between the two types is by conducting an EVP session or attempting to provoke the entity into interacting with the investigators.

Theories related to why human entities exist include:

- They have some sort of unfinished business and are in need of assistance.

- They're here as the result of a traumatic event such as murder or being a casualty of war.

- They died suddenly and don't realize they are dead

The above theories were founded based on small bits and pieces of information collected over the years from countless investigations. The truth is we really don't have concrete evidence to support any of them but overall they have been embraced by most researchers in the field.

Elementals

There are many theories related to this type of entity. At one time Elementals were thought to be demons, but this is no longer the case based on general consensus among most paranormal researchers. The characteristic commonly agreed upon by most researchers is that Elementals are not and never were human. Elementals are often referred to as nature spirits and are believed to inhabit and protect nature. Entities of this nature are believed to be inquisitive and sometimes aggressive. Elementals are believed to belong to one of the four elements:

Earth	Swiss alchemist Paracelsus classified Gnomes as earth elementals. He describes them as two spans high, very reluctant to interact with humans, and able to move through solid earth as easily as humans move through air.
Fire	Salamanders – Although spelled the same, these elementals are not to be confused with amphibian salamanders. The Element Encyclopedia of Magical Creatures cites the salamander to be a poisonous beast of mythology.
Water	Undines appear in European folklore as fairy-like creatures; the name may be used interchangeably with those of other water spirits.
Air	Sylphs are described as invisible beings of the air or elementals of air by Swiss alchemist Paracelsus.

During Medieval times the belief in elementals was widely accepted and highly influential in medieval natural philosophy. Many believe that entities of this nature are fairies, pixies, gnomes and even leprechauns.

Demons

Demonic entities are believed to be malevolent, unclean spirits that have the ability to possess humans. The belief in the existence of demons is widely accepted among Christian, Jewish and Arabic cultures. One difference in the opinion of demons is the Arabic culture believes that demons can be both good and evil, and they refer to them as "jinn".

Most paranormal researchers agree that if one encounters a haunting where there is suspected demonic activity, it is in everyone's best interest to seek qualified assistance from the Church to help resolve the matter. Many feel that the only truly qualified organization to intercede in a demonic haunting or possession is the Catholic Church. One little known fact about the Catholic Church is that although all priests are trained in performing exorcisms, the Vatican only allows one priest in every diocese to perform the ritual. The identity of that priest is closely guarded and the authorization must come from Rome.

Theories Related to Paranormal Activity

Up to this point we have discussed theories related to the types of entities that you may encounter while conducting a paranormal investigation. We are now going to shift our discussion to the theories related to the types of activity that one may encounter during a paranormal investigation.

Like all living creatures on this planet we rely heavily on our five senses; sight, hearing, smell, touch and taste when interpreting the world around us. From a scientific standpoint there is an inherent problem with this as not everyone interprets everything the same way. One individual's vision or hearing may be better than another. Therefore, one person may feel something and describe it one way while another person who feels the exact same thing may describe it as something else. This is the primary reason that the scientific community mandates that scientific data and methods related to their research must be archived so that others can gain access to it to test the data and methods in order to build on the research that has been done.

With that said it is easy to understand why paranormal researchers have struggled to gain credibility within the scientific community. There are countless video and audio recordings floating around the World Wide Web that the original publishers claim contains proof of the existence of ghosts or spirits. Most of these contain mysterious voices or sounds that seem out of place. Some depict anomalous readings obtained on hand held EMF meters (see figure 1.3) during question and answer sessions. Some even contain what appear to be objects moving on their own. What does this all mean? It means absolutely nothing because the evidence being presented is considered anecdotal at best, given the fact that most researchers do not take the time to document the methods that are related to the details associated with the data presented.

Most researchers are working off of theories that are either widely accepted or variations of these theories based on their research. While this is all well and good, the main problem with the evidence or data being presented is that it lacks the supporting details that would go a long way towards improving its credibility.

Poltergeist Theory

While this book is dedicated to the scientific method as it pertains to paranormal research, the theory related to poltergeist activity is worth mentioning. This theory is highly controversial and pertains to a type of activity that one may encounter during an investigation. The term poltergeist is derived from the German word *poltern*, meaning "to rumble or make a noise" and *Geist*, meaning "ghost or spirit" and simply means noisy spirit. While the true nature of the source of activity is agreed to stem from the living, the activity that is associated with the theory is not as cut and dry. Most are in agreement that the source of the activity is generally tied to a single person occupying a dwelling, usually being a young female. With respect to the activity itself there are two general schools of thought. One suggests the poltergeist phenomena itself may stem from an individuals ESP abilities, while the other suggests that the activity is a result of a spirit or ghost reacting to the individual.

Did You Know?

ESP is an abbreviation for the term extrasensory perception. Perception of information about events, that is external and previously unknown to one's self, through means beyond the normal five senses. Telepathy, clairvoyance and precognition are examples of psychic abilities in this category.

Theories Related to the Environment

There are many theories out there related to how entities are either energized by the environment or related to their ability to affect the environment around them. Theories revolving around such topics as ionization, temperature changes, static electricity, humidity, lightning, solar storms, and gamma bursts have been debated for some time. In order to effectively cover each of these subjects in detail it would take many chapters and is beyond the scope of this book, however we will touch on each to give you a general understanding of the theory associated with them.

The primary idea that supports the basis for each of the following theories revolves around the concept that paranormal entities derive their ability to interact on our physical plane from some form of energy. The exact nature and source of this energy is still unknown, but it is believed that this energy source can be either natural or manmade.

PARANORMAL THEORIES

Theories Related to EMF

EMF, or Electromagnetic Fields, are physical fields created by electrically charged objects. Objects such as electric power lines, alarm clocks and even the planet we live on produce EMF fields.

There are two controversial theories in the paranormal community related to EMF. One suggests that entities have the ability to affect or produce EMF fields and as such paranormal researchers can detect or track these entities using handheld EMF meters. The other theory, which is more controversial than the first, suggests that researchers may be able to communicate with entities by using a specific type of EMF meter called a K-II or some other variation of an EMF meter that works under the same principle of the K-II.

Figure 1.3
Deluxe K-II EMF Meter

Did You Know?

When the K-II meter is exposed to a magnetic field, an electrical current is induced within the device's circuitry and the relative strength of the field is visually displayed on a scale of 5-LED lights. The K-II is only capable of measuring electromagnetic fields from 30 – 20,000 Hz.

While we will agree that there is no hard evidence to support these theories, we can tell you that we have had more than one compelling experience that would support these claims. On one case in particular, we were able to get very convincing responses on a K-II meter which was stationary on the floor in the middle of the room. We verbally asked the entity to approach the meter to give us a sign of its presence and the meter went off. Being the warm and fuzzy skeptics we are, we repeated this process at least a dozen times with the same results. We were actually able to witness this force illuminate the meter to specific levels by simply asking during two separate investigations.

While there are many paranormal researchers that have downplayed or even denounced the K-II meter because they feel it is too sensitive and easily produce false positives, we feel that if used correctly the K-II has its place in paranormal research. It is very important that each and every one of you take the time to learn how to use each piece of equipment that you own in addition to understanding their limits and known flaws. We never rely on the K-II alone and always deploy additional EMF meters of different types to validate our readings. We will go into more detail about the K-II as well as other equipment used for paranormal research in chapter six.

Manmade Energy Sources

Manmade energy sources are those which are produced from sources such as A/C power lines, electronics and transmission signals generated from electronic devices. Such devices include cell phones and radio or television broadcast signals, right down to the walkie-talkies that one may use during an investigation.

Numerous reports have been documented regarding investigators experiencing battery drain on equipment such as a camcorders or digital cameras during an investigation just prior to witnessing or experiencing some sort of elevated paranormal activity. These reports are key to support the theory that spirits require energy to manifest or manipulate the environment around them.

PARANORMAL THEORIES

Natural Energy Sources

When it comes to natural energy sources which a paranormal entity may draw power from there are endless possibilities. We mentioned several of these earlier and now we will elaborate on them and the theory associated with them.

Ionization – Weather events such as thunderstorms charge the surrounding atmosphere with negative ions. But what are ions and how are they related to paranormal investigations?

In its most basic definition an ion is an atom or molecule in which the total number of electrons is not equal to the total number of protons and results in either a positive or negative electrical charge. The energy required to detach an electron from a molecule, in this case atmospheric gas, is supplied by lightning strikes. When a lightning strike occurs it creates a massive influx of electrons in the atmosphere that overloads atmospheric molecules with free electrons causing them to become ions. Based on research, which was published by Dr. Klaus Heinemann in his book entitled "The Orb Project", paranormal entities are thought to be able to draw on the energy resulting from an increase in negative ions at a location. As a result many paranormal investigators will utilize ion meters during their investigation in an attempt to establish a correlation, and validate the theory between any paranormal activity witnessed and the associated ion reading.

Temperature Changes – Cold spots, while naturally occurring, are believed to be associated with paranormal activity when they are isolated to a specific location or small area within that location. The theory is based on the assumption that paranormal entities are able to draw energy from the air that surrounds them which results in a temperature drop, in order to manifest or to manipulate objects around them. Based on this theory paranormal investigators will employ one or more instruments that are able to record ambient temperature readings.

Static Electricity / Humidity / Lightning – Each of these are environmental conditions believed to be relevant to an entity's ability to absorb energy from its surroundings and are closely related to the Ionization theory. Essentially researchers believe that spirits or entities are better able to derive energy from the environment when these conditions are either present or at elevated levels in order to manifest or manipulate objects.

Solar Storms, Magnetic Storms and Gamma Bursts – Each of these events are magnetic in nature and have a direct impact on EMF fields on our planet. The theory behind these events suggests that they may be a catalyst for increased paranormal activity based on the idea that paranormal entities are either able to draw energy from EMF sources or are affected by them.

Everything Else – The truth of the matter is there are so many theories out there that attempt to link paranormal activity to the elements of nature that one could write several books solely dedicated to the few that we have discussed so far.

Summary

With everything that we have discussed up to this point it is easy to deduce we as paranormal investigators must make it a priority to research every detail available to us about a site that we investigate. We also need to record baseline readings for everything that we have the ability to measure. By doing so, each and every one of us has the capability to either validate or improve on many of the theories that exist related to the paranormal thus substantiating these theories and lending credibility to the field of paranormal research.

3

WHAT ARE WE AFTER HERE?

The Holy Grail has been the subject of countless stories spanning thousands of years while its legend has mystified many civilizations the world over. What does the Holy Grail have to do with the subject matter of this chapter? Simple, in addition to the obvious religious meaning associated with the Holy Grail, the Holy Grail is also considered a metaphor which signifies the ultimate prize at the end of a quest. Isn't that what each and every one of us involved in the paranormal research field is doing, seeking irrefutable proof of the paranormal?

Today the metaphoric grail may symbolize something different for each and every one of us involved in paranormal research. At one time it was believed that video footage of an apparition was considered the most coveted piece of evidence one could ever hope to obtain during his/her research endeavors. While we would love to have the opportunity to investigate a location where that type of evidence is captured, the simple fact is that advances in technology have made it possible for the average high school student to produce video special effects that would make Steven Spielberg envious. It's no wonder people are skeptical when it comes to the validity of some of the evidence being released these days.

We as human beings rely heavily on our five senses to process the environment around us, so it is no surprise that much of the evidence paranormal researchers are working diligently to obtain is centered on them. Many in the field have digital thermometers, audio recorders, and countless types of video recording equipment which they lug from location to location in a feeble attempt to capture something they hope will help shed some light on the field that we study. Prior to the technology available today, researchers were armed with nothing more than analog tape recorders and 35mm film-based cameras (which some folks still prefer today) as they headed out to locations with reported claims of activity.

While much of the evidence that we are after today is still based on the five human senses - sight, hearing, taste, touch, and smell - the increase in the availability of high tech devices has broadened the search to include other forms of evidence as well. In this chapter we will discuss each of the types of evidence that we are looking for and how to document it.

Visual Based Evidence

The old adage "a picture is worth a thousand words" has never been more true when it comes to paranormal research. Researchers the world over are pushing the envelope with regards to the number and types of cameras they are using during their research. When it comes to visual-based evidence, paranormal researchers use a varied combination of devices in an attempt to capture anything out of the ordinary.

Visual based evidence ranges from ordinary objects that seem to move on their own, to full blown apparitions that have been witnessed walking through walls. The following list covers most visual based evidence believed to be possible.

Apparitions

An apparition is defined as the projection or manifestation of a quasi-physical entity. Theories abound regarding the types, purpose, and even classification that an apparition may have, but to be honest, this is all speculation and unfounded. We will focus the subject of this topic on what you may witness or capture on film during a paranormal investigation, leaving the proposed theories for another time. There have been countless documented reports from all over the world where people either seen or captured on film many different types of apparitions. Reports have described apparitions ranging from partial to full bodied formations that appear to look as real as anyone you may know, to various lesser translucent forms. There have also been reports which describe apparitions as nothing more than a dark silhouette; these are commonly referred to as shadow people.

Orbs and Mists

Orbs and mists are another form of commonly reported anomaly by many paranormal researchers. This form of evidence has become heavily debated over the last decade based on the fact that these anomalies seem to be easily reproduced in the right conditions. Explanations for this type of anomaly involve the cameras flash in combination with anything ranging from dust or moisture in the air, to flying insects. The controversy has literally divided the field to form two distinct groups consisting of those who totally ignore any type of evidence related to orbs or mist on one side, and those who feel this type of evidence should not be overlooked. Proponents for orb and mist evidence received a huge boost for their cause when two well know and accredited Ph.D.'s, Klaus Heinemann and Micheal Ledwith, published a book entitled "The Orb Project".

Object Manipulation

This particular type of visual evidence is one of our favorite and involves the use of one or more video cameras, preferably stationary, that captures an object, such as a door, chair, or table lamp moving unassisted. Skeptics maintain that this form of evidence is easily discredited given the fact that we are generally only presented with a single angle of the anomaly, and the fact that this type of evidence is the easiest form of which to create a hoax. While researchers have no way of predicting any type of activity, they should take measures during their equipment setup to ensure that any evidence captured on video has multiple angles and detailed records to support the evidence.

Light Anomalies

Light anomalies are another form of visual evidence some maintain may have paranormal origins. This form of anomaly generally involves unexplained flashes of light in an area of total darkness and upon investigation witnesses are unable to locate a potential light source. The light produced from this type of anomaly can range in intensity as small as a dime, to enough light to fully illuminate a room. These anomalies have been witnessed and documented indoors as well as outdoors, and have been reported world wide.

Audio Based Evidence

Evidence of this nature is based on sound and ranges from unexplained knocks and bumps to spoken words. The acronym EVP stands for electronic voice phenomena, and refers to the process of capturing disembodied voices or sounds on a digital or analog audio recorder. Another form of audio based evidence is called Direct Voice Phenomenon and was once primarily associated with mediums and séances. Today the term is used to describe any unexplained sound that is audibly heard by the unassisted human ear while conducting a paranormal investigation. As stated earlier, the sounds can range from foot steps to words and are classified under one of the following classifications that were originally established by Sara Estep, founder of the American Association of Electronic Voice Phenomena:

Class A EVP – "Loud and Clear. No headphones are required." (Estep, 2008) This type of EVP is easily discernable and everyone who hears it is able to identify it with no guidance or instruction.

Class B EVP – "louder and clearer and can often be heard without headphones." (Estep, 2008) This type of EVP, while louder and clearer than a Class C, often requires the use of headphones to hear. Another characteristic of the classification is you are not able to decipher all of the words or sounds on the recording.

WHAT ARE WE AFTER HERE?

Class C EVP – "Faint whispery voices that require headphones to hear them and rarely can all the words be interpreted." (Estep, 2008) This type of EVP is the most prevalent; its characteristics include whispers or unrecognizable sounds. Often with this type of EVP researchers are only able to decipher just enough to indicate that what has been captured is out of place.

Some paranormal researchers have taken upon themselves to expand upon Sara Estep's original classification system by adding additional classifications and attempting to expand each criteria. In addition to the attempts to expand the classification system, others have added to the confusion by attempting to assign acronyms to the sounds heard and even the method used to hear them. While these expanded classification systems may serve those groups or individuals well, the lack of standardization does little more than add to the confusion that exists in a field already full of controversy.

Taste, Touch, and Smell

Any type of evidence that falls under this category really amounts to nothing more than a personal experience or speculation. Often this sort of phenomena involves one or more investigators experiencing an odor, cold spot, or the feeling of being touched during an investigation.

Given the nature of the experience it is difficult at best to document evidence of this nature, with the exception of cold spots, due to the power of suggestion. The power of suggestion is the psychological process by which one person may guide the thoughts, feelings, or behavior of another with nothing more than a simple suggestion. We are not saying that this type of evidence should be ignored in any way, we are only pointing out the inherent issues that are associated with them.

One method that has proven beneficial in recording evidence of this nature is to implement the protocol that each investigator carries and maintains a personal case log during the investigation in which the investigator records these types of experiences as they happen. The record should include actual time, location, the names of who was present, and the exact location of each person to the proximity of the investigator. The logs are then turned in at the end of the investigation and compared during the evidence review process. By doing so you are able to track the occurrences and the evidence gained is more credible.

Temperature is the only exception as it is easily documented with an ambient thermometer. The significance of temperature drops in relation to paranormal activity stems from the theory that entities draw energy from their surroundings in order to manifest, thereby resulting in lower air temperatures around them. While "cold spots" are explainable by naturally occurring events, there is a possibility that when accompanied by other unknown phenomena in the same vicinity they can be linked, thereby helping to support the theory.

Other Types of Evidence

Up to this point we have only discussed evidence that is based on the five human senses. With advances in technology some paranormal investigators are making a case that there may be a correlation linking the level of paranormal activity to specific environmental conditions at a location. Many investigators are using instruments which are used to measure such things as electromagnetic field, ion levels, humidity, and barometric pressure while incorporating the data into their investigations in an attempt to verify these theories.

A Different Approach

One concept, while not new, is for investigators to attempt to "chain" evidence together in an attempt to give the evidence more credibility and make it more difficult for skeptics to simply dismiss. This process requires either access to a large inventory of equipment or involves multiple investigations of a single location in order to compile enough data to solidly support the claims. While it is very common for paranormal research groups to investigate a location multiple times if permitted, the process is very expensive and time consuming. Coupled with the fact that most paranormal research groups are under funded and under equipped the task is daunting sometimes, to say the least.

One approach that our group uses to help overcome these issues in an attempt to get the most out of each investigation is to deploy data loggers in each area of a location. We were fortunate enough to have established a good working relationship with a company that specializes in producing equipment geared specifically for scientific research. The only reason we are mentioning the company is the fact that they offer a unique product in their line of data logging equipment. While there are many companies producing and selling data logging equipment, Fourier manufactures and distributes a product called the MultiLogPRO. The MultiLogPRO is unique in the fact that this device has the ability to handle up to eight simultaneous inputs and is configurable with a wide selection of probes tailored to meet just about everyone's needs. The units that we use are configured to measure EMF, temperature, relative humidity, and sound levels. The unit can operate in a stand alone mode measuring and recording readings to its internal memory, or connected to a laptop or PC where the data is streamed directly to the PCs hard drive. We prefer using ours connected to laptops as it allows us to monitor each unit from our headquarters in real time via Microsoft's RDP protocol. Compared to other data logging equipment on the market Fourier equipment is reasonably priced as well. If you would like more information on the Fourier line of equipment you can check them out on the World Wide Web at http://www.fourier-sys.com. This isn't intended to be a shameless plug and we don't receive any compensation or discounts for sending folks their way. We just feel they offer a quality product that works well for paranormal research.

Note! *For your convenience we have included an extensive list of vendors following chapter ten. This list is intended to help you find reputable suppliers for goods and services related to paranormal investigation.*

Environmental Variables

So far in this chapter we have only talked about evidence related to paranormal activity. In chapter two we discussed theories related to the environment and the possible impact those enviromental conditions may have on the phenomena that we are attempting to document. We also touched on the fact that many of the theories related to the environment are still unproven.

You will often find information documented by paranormal groups that indicated things such as moon phase, EMF readings, magnetic field data, ion counts, and current weather conditions at the time of their investigation. While this information alone will not indicate the presence of paranormal activity, groups who base there investigations on the scientific method record this data in an attempt to identify trends in the data that may indicate that there is some relationship between the conditions being monitored and the level of activity being experienced.

Some groups, such as ours, go beyond the above stated data sets and gather geological data related to the sites they are investigating. The information they include consists of the mineral content of the soil, radiation levels, and geological formations surrounding the investigation site. All of this is done in and attempt to correlate specific geological conditions with the level of paranormal activity associated with the site.

Summary

When utilizing the scientific method for paranormal research, the more data you collect to support your theory the better. Always steer clear of questionable techniques when collecting data. Remember, while it is encouraged to think outside of the box when forming theories, it is very important to focus you data collection efforts on sound principals and techniques.

4

SKILLS NEEDED FOR SUCESS

Regardless of why or how you conduct your paranormal investigations, most paranormal researchers will agree there are a core set of skills each member of the team is required to have in order to be successful in this field. While many of these skills apply to other aspects of our lives, our intention is to show you how they apply to being a successful paranormal research investigator.

We will approach this by breaking the skill sets down as they apply to specific roles within a paranormal research team and then detail how each skill set applies to the paranormal research field.

Skills Required by All Members

Observational Skills

Observational skills are the cornerstone of paranormal research. The reason for this is that the scientific method is the process of making observations and asking questions based on those observations, and then forming theories for which we conduct experiments in an attempt to validate said theories. Observational skills are critical to forming theories; each team member will need to hone this skill due to the fact that many times the equipment used during investigations will not be in the right place to capture an anomaly that is witnessed.

Time Management

Time management is a skill set that each team member must master. Most of us have room for improvement, and this skill is essential to producing consistent and well documented evidence. Paranormal research is all about observation, and as such, we need to be able to recreate the events of an investigation down to the minute. It is essential that all members of the investigation team are able to manage time as well as document proceedings of an investigation in the context of time as it is critical in reconstructing events after an investigation.

Communication Skills

Communication skills are fundamental to every investigation as everyone involved must be able to convey what they have seen, heard or felt. Communication skills apply to both verbal and written communication, but are particularly important when it comes to documenting the details of a case, or recording the proceedings of the investigation, as well as conversing with your client.

Problem Solving Skills

Problem solving skills are important to paranormal research as one should always attempt to find a plausible explanation for any anomaly that is witnessed or experienced. Problem solving skills allow us to apply logic and reason during the validation phase of an investigation, which is the process of identifying possible explanations for what may have been witnessed or experienced, and then attempting to apply those explanations to the current situation.

Organizational Skills

Organizational skills are a key factor for success in life as well as paranormal research. These skills can be thought of as the "glue" that holds everything together, and are considered necessary for each investigator to manage themselves effectively and efficiently during an investigation. Many times while reviewing evidence the situation will arise where everyone present during the investigation must be accounted for in order to rule out the possibility of contamination in an effort to validate the evidence.

Required Skills for Founders and Directors

Leadership Skills

Leadership skills are a key factor for the success of any paranormal research team. If you are unable to motivate and direct your team then chaos is the best you can hope for. Leadership skills refer to one's ability to direct his or her group's efforts in an attempt to obtain a common goal. "A leader is one who knows the way, goes the way, and shows the way." ~ John C. Maxwell

Team Building

Team building is a skill set that refers to one's ability to bring a group of people together and focus their efforts on a common goal or purpose. This skill is essential for the founder or director of a group to master in order to maintain team morale. Many teams operate on a voluntary basis and therefore it is up to the founder or director of the group to keep each member motivated and involved in order to minimize member turnover.

Personnel Management Skills

Personnel Management refers to the skills needed to direct, train and manage the members of your team. Some team members may require extra training or instruction, especially regarding the use of equipment or investigation technique, which may be new to them. It is the duty of the founder or director to exercise patience and provide the necessary guidance for success. Personnel management skills are essential to developing a well rounded organization. This skill set works hand in hand with team building and is essential to reducing team member turnover. Given the amount of effort that goes into training your members, it is in your best interest to develop these skills to help cope with the diversity and dynamics of your group.

Typical Roles within a Paranormal Research Group

Regardless of what approach or methods a paranormal research group employs during investigations, there is one thing that most teams have in common and that is the structure of their organization. While some groups may have people who perform multiple functions within the group, the following roles are generally found in every paranormal research group.

Founder / Director

While some groups choose to use the title of founder and others director, the role within the group is the same. The Founder or Director is generally the person or individuals who started the group, and are responsible for building the team as well as establishing all policies and procedures. This individual has final say over all aspects related to the group.

Case Manager

The case manager is the individual who is responsible for managing and coordinating all events and resources leading up to the investigation. The individual serving in this role requires all of the skill sets that we previously discussed given they interact with clients as well as the team, and are responsible for scheduling and coordinating all aspects prior to the investigation.

Tech Manager

The tech manager is the individual who is primarily in charge of equipment setup, testing, and research. While the individual serving in this role may participate as an investigator on a case, they are primarily responsible for monitoring the equipment during the investigation as well as training other team members on equipment setup and use.

Investigator

Investigators are team members whose primary responsibility is to observe and validate claims that have been reported relating to the activity surrounding a case. Investigators may also do background research related to the history of the location being investigated.

Summary

As stated earlier, many groups have individuals who often serve in multiple roles within a group. There are also groups who may have more specialized roles within their organization depending on the number of members they may have. While the roles that we have covered are not all inclusive, they are considered core roles that can be found in every paranormal team.

5

TYPES OF INVESTIGATORS AND THEIR METHODS

Up to this point we have talked about the supernatural realm and how the field of paranormal study relates to it. We have covered some of the numerous theories that are associated with our understanding of paranormal activity. This brings us to the topic of this chapter, Investigation Methods and Types of Investigators.

Merriam-Webster defines the term method as follows:

"**Method** - a way, technique, or process of or for doing something which implies an orderly logical arrangement usually in steps."

Main Entry:	meth·od
Function:	*noun*
Etymology:	Middle English, prescribed treatment, from Latin methodus, from Greek methodos, from meta- + hodos way
Date of origin:	15th century

TYPES OF INVESTIGATORS AND THEIR METHODS

Alternative Methods

While the area of concentration in this chapter will focus on the scientific method and how it should be applied to paranormal research, it is very important to understand that there are alternative methods being used in the field today. As stated in the definition above, the term method implies an orderly logical arrangement of steps used to accomplish a task or goal, which indicates that logic must be associated with any method. The problem with logic, which is a mode of reasoning, is it can either be viewed as valid or faulty depending on who is analyzing the outcome.

"Logic - The art of thinking and reasoning in strict accordance with the limitations and incapacities of the human misunderstanding."
- *Ambrose Briece* (1842-1914)

In a previous chapter we already pointed out that the paranormal research field is teeming with controversy and assumption, so why would one think the methods used to investigate claims of the paranormal are any different?

Skeptics Point of View

As far as the scientific community is concerned, paranormal researchers employ questionable methods to investigate the paranormal. These methods can range from the use of psychics or mediums in an attempt to locate, identify, and communicate with entities from the other side, to using state of the art electronics such as an EMF meter, originally developed and intended for another use, to measure and confirm the presence of a reported entity. Some investigators have even combined these techniques to produce varied and questionable results. The bottom line is you can't base your knowledge of the paranormal or the methods used to investigate it from what you may have seen on TV. Much of the controversy related to paranormal investigation methods stems from the individuals conducting the research and their lack of knowledge towards applying the methods or using the equipment properly.

This lack of standardization with regards to the methods used to investigate the paranormal has only resulted in fueling the flames of controversy and providing skeptics with valid points to aid their cause for dismissing the existence of just about everything produced from researchers in the paranormal field. Now, add to the paradox the countless faked images and EVP recordings that have been circulated, and it's no wonder those of us in the field have a difficult time gaining acceptance of the research that we do. Include the bickering that sometimes exists and the various tactics some use to discredit others in an attempt to elevate their own status in the field; it is very easy to understand why advances in the paranormal research field have been slow to non-existent.

There is no denying that there are quite a few labels floating around the paranormal research field that attempt to classify the many types of researchers and the methods they use. As the founders of our own paranormal research team, we feel that nothing is gained by labeling or condemning others techniques or view points. While we may not agree with some of the methods used or how some individuals approach an investigation, we absolutely do not condone expressing anything in a negative light publicly. This establishes a negative connotation for everyone involved.

Types of Investigators

We feel that investigators in the field fall under one of two types. First are thrill seekers: those individuals or groups that are merely in the field for the excitement and adrenalin rush they get from going in to a reported haunted location. Second are professionals, those who always maintain a courteous and professional attitude thereby establishing a positive persona for all involved in the paranormal field. In the event you did not pick up on it, our opinion related to the classification of researcher has nothing to do with the methods they choose to employ during their investigations and everything to do with the way they conduct themselves and the positive reputation they establish with the general public. Granted, one could argue that the type of investigator you are is solely dictated by the methods you choose to employ during your paranormal investigations. However, most people involved in this field would agree that many of us have used a blend of methods at one point in time. Given the fact that we know so little with regards to the paranormal, who can honestly say one method or belief is the most credible. Based on the current state of affairs in the paranormal field one has to ask how we ever expect to see light at the end of the tunnel. Most paranormal researchers will agree that the primary issue with most methods employed to investigate claims of the paranormal stem from a lack of standards that dictate how these methods should be applied. Another problem related to most of the methods has to do with the individuals attempting to apply them without fully understanding the methods.

The matters above are not intended to discourage anyone from getting involved in the paranormal research field. Our intention is only to point out some of the more prevalent issues and controversies that exist in the field today. In fact, these are all matters that we became aware of during the process of forming our group, which is one of the primary reasons we chose to approach our research using the scientific method. When we began researching what information was available on the World Wide Web to assist individuals such as ourselves in breaking into the field, we found a lot of inconsistent information outlining many aspects related to accepted standards. We quickly noticed the diversity in the methods being used with respect to how an investigation should be approached and carried out. We noticed a lot of groups proclaiming their use of scientific based equipment which was of interest to us, but few really elaborated on the methods they employed with regards to using the equipment.

The Scientific Method

The logical choice for us was attempting to adapt our approach to paranormal research using the scientific method. In order to accomplish this, one needs to have a thorough understanding of the scientific method before attempting to apply it to any field of study, especially paranormal research. The scientific method is nothing more than the process of asking a question and then attempting to answer said question by making observations. The observations lead to theories, and the theories require experiments that attempt to validate those theories. The more formal definition of the scientific method as stated by Merriam-Webster states "The Scientific method consists of forming principles and procedures for the systematic pursuit of knowledge involving the recognition and formulation of a problem, the collection of data through observation and experiment, and the formulation and testing of hypotheses"

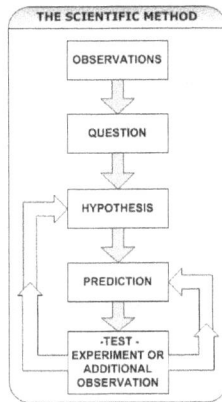

Figure 1.4 Flowchart depicting the Scientific Method

Sounds easy enough, right? Well the biggest oversight that we feel most researchers in the paranormal field make is they tend to ask too broad a question. For example, if we ask the question "Do ghosts exist?" and apply the scientific method in an attempt to answer it, one would quickly become overwhelmed or severely criticized. The primary reason for this is the vast number of inconsistent variables that are associated with the paranormal realm as well as much of the anecdotal evidence produced to date. In order to apply the scientific method to answer any question we need to remember to narrow and focus our question to specific areas related to the paranormal and take great care to avoid assumptions.

This is a daunting task to say the least given there are no hard facts that support many of the claims and theories that exist at present. So what do we make of all the eyewitness accounts, photos, and video evidence that has been presented to date? As far as the scientific community is concerned the evidence or data produced to date is nothing more than anecdotal. However, those of us in the field should not discount the data that has been recorded to date since paranormal evidence is scarce and unpredictable.

Applying the Scientific Method

We have talked in detail about the problems paranormal researchers face during their investigations and what the scientific method can do to help. Now let's take it one step further by providing an example. We have discussed in great detail the different types of evidence that paranormal investigators are attempting to capture in chapter three, but for this example we will apply the scientific method while attempting to validate a captured EVP.

EVP stands for electronic voice phenomena, and refers to the process of capturing disembodied voices or sounds on a digital or analog audio recorder. It is important to keep an open mind yet remain somewhat skeptical when applying the scientific method during your research endeavors. We must always question the evidence that we capture in an attempt to eliminate all known natural causes which some investigators refer to as debunking.

For this exercise we have created a simple floor plan which depicts a single family home. The clients that live in this home have reported the following claims which they feel are paranormal in nature:

- Sounds of foot steps are heard in the hallway late at night when everyone is in bed.

- Voices are heard in the two bedrooms furthest from the living room.

- Unexplained banging noises.

- Doors open on their own.

Take a moment to review the sample floor plan (figure 1.5) that we have provided for this exercise. We have placed symbols on the floor plan to illustrate the typical equipment setup that our group employs during our investigations. The Key below will help identify each piece of equipment being used:

 Represents Digital Audio Recorder

 Represents Close Circuit TV Camera

 Represents Data Logger

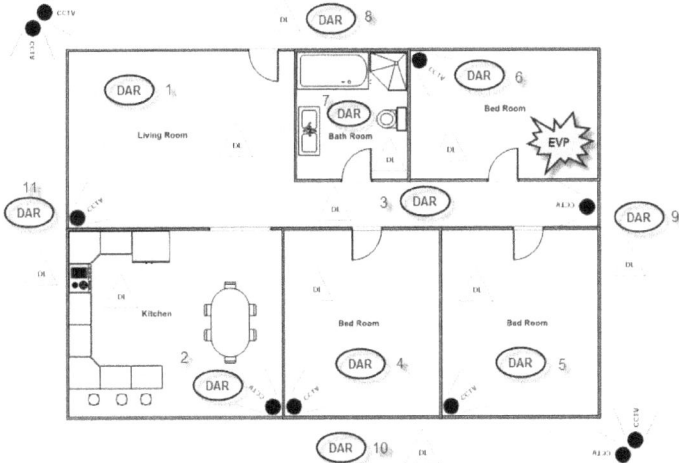

Figure 1.5 – Applying the Scientific Method to Paranormal Research Exercise

45

Our team uses both stationary and hand held infrared video cameras as well as a full spectrum video camera. For this exercise we are only focusing on the stationary equipment depicted in the illustration which consists of ten data loggers that record temperature, EMF, humidity and decibel level, eleven stationary digital audio recorders as well as the ten close circuit TV cameras. While reviewing the floor plan please take note of the fact that in addition to the equipment that is set up inside the reported location, we also have equipment setup and running that covers all four sides of the structure from the outside. This setup should be mandatory for any group conducting research as it helps identify most of the false positives captured during an investigation which greatly increases the validity of the evidence you do capture.

Did You Know? *Infrared light or, IR light as it is sometimes called, lies between the visible and microwave portions of the electromagnetic spectrum. Infrared Video Light enables us to film in near and absolute darkness. The infrared LEDs act as an invisible light source that can not be seen by the human eye but can be seen by your camcorder.*

We realize that the amount of equipment needed to cover a typical single family home like this requires a significant monetary investment. But remember you don't have to purchase everything at once. If you intend to base your investigations on the scientific method it should be something that you strive for. The benefits of covering all four sides of the home externally are as follows:

- We are able to rule out outside contamination on any EVP's captured inside the home.

- We can monitor and track all outside movement around the home, which helps us validate any anomalies captured inside the home.

- We can compare the external and internal readings with the same time stamp in an effort to validate any anomalous readings captured inside the home. We use this in an attempt to validate the hypothesis that paranormal entities have the ability to affect EMF fields.

One of the negatives to adding external equipment as well as increased coverage inside the home is it adds a significant amount of time to the review process. We feel the increased time to review all of the data captured is well worth it as the data we capture will prove worth its weight in gold when it comes to validating the claims and proving many of the theories that exist in the paranormal field.

During the review process we discover what we believe is an EVP that was captured on DAR #6 in one of the bed rooms. The EVP is a direct response to the question "Can you tell us your name?" and the response is a resounding "NO!" The EVP response is clearly heard and does not require any modification or enhancement to be heard. It is agreed by all that the voice recorded belongs to none of the team members present at the time it was captured. This type of EVP is considered a "Class A" EVP by the paranormal field.

Did You Know? | *Electronic Voice Phenomena is classified under one of three classifications that were originally established by Sara Estep. The classifications are Class A, Class B, and Class C. See chapter three for a complete explanation of the classification system.*

Based on the fact that we have taken the necessary steps during our pre-investigation equipment setup by placing cameras, digital audio recorders, and data loggers outside the home to help rule out any possibility of external contamination, we simply need to review the data captured by the outside equipment to confirm that this EVP was not from an outside source. Our next step is to review the data captured by the equipment in the adjoining rooms to see if the EVP was recorded on any of that equipment as well. For the sake of this exercise we reviewed the data on all equipment used during the investigation and the EVP was only recorded by DAR #6 and the hand held infrared camera that was present during the EVP session in the bedroom.

Now that we have reviewed all of the data captured during the investigation and have isolated our EVP, it is time to apply the scientific method in an attempt to either reveal possible sources or validate that we may have a genuine paranormal event.

The first step was to review the data captured during our investigation which is considered the observation phase of the scientific method. The next step is to formulate a question or series of questions based on the results of our observation:

Question: What was the source of word "No!" that was recorded?

→ We are able to eliminate all outside sources based on our review of our external audio recorders.

→ We are able to rule out electronic contamination; from such sources as radio broadcasts or cell phone tower bleed through based on the fact the DAR #6 and the hand held camcorder were the only two devices that captured the word "No!"

→ We are able to rule out that the word "No!" was a result of one of our team members speaking during the session based on the CCTV footage recorded during the time of the EVP session.

We now need to form a hypothesis in an attempt to derive an answer to our question.

Fact: Based on the fact that we are unable to determine a source for the audible response we received to our question we need to consider the following possibilities:

→ The source of the response may have been some sort of undetected electronic interference.

→ The source of the response may not be the word "No!" but instead could be what some psychologists refer to as pareidolia. Pareidolia is a term used to describe the process of forming words out of sounds based on the power of suggestion.

→ The source of the response may have been paranormal in nature.

We now have three hypotheses to follow up on. We will need to devise tests that will either validate or disprove at least two of the three hypotheses that we derived in order to focus our research.

- For the first hypotheses "undetected electronic interference" we need to take steps to eliminate any possible form of electronic contamination. This is easily done with the use of a faraday cage. During our next visit to this location we will place the digital voice recorder in a mini-faraday cage and repeat the EVP session by asking the same questions in an attempt to record the same response that was captured the first time.

Did You Know?

The English scientist Michael Faraday invented an enclosure comprised of conductive material which blocks out external static electric fields in 1863. These enclosures are used to block external broadcast signals from reaching electronic devices placed within.

- For the second hypothesis we will attempt to rule out the possibility of pareidolia by seeking the opinions of multiple people who were not involved in the initial investigation without any predisposition. We will track their responses in an attempt to trend the data we receive from their feedback.

- The last hypothesis, a paranormal source, is the most difficult to prove. Since we are not able to validate the existence of spirits or entities at this time, we can only wait for the results from the first two tests before we spend any more time on this.

Once we are able to disprove the other two hypotheses, we can then start looking at the other data that was recorded during this session in an attempt to identify other anomalies that may have occurred at the same time.

Did You Know?

Pareidolia is a psychological phenomenon used to explain such acts as seeing images of animals or faces in clouds or hearing hidden messages on records played in reverse. Other paranormal groups use the term matrixing to describe the pareidolia phenomenon.

If the data warrants it, we need to repeat the cycle as many times as necessary in order to derive the root cause. We will discuss the basics for conducting solid paranormal investigation in great detail in chapter eight, but based on this exercise we just went through it should be very apparent that record keeping is essential to a successful investigation. It is imperative that you synchronize all time pieces prior to starting the investigation. This will greatly assist you during the review process when attempting to reconstruct the events of the evening.

Summary

Using the scientific method during your investigation requires a great deal of work with respect to preparation, planning, placement of your equipment, and impeccable record keeping. It also significantly increases the amount of equipment that a team needs in order to adequately cover and record data at a location during the investigation. For those who are willing to make the investment the return is solid evidence and a better understanding of the data captured, which is hands down the best method for gaining credibility in the scientific community.

Did You Know? *Paranormal activity is often witnessed during daylight hours and there is no reason an active investigation can't take place during the day. The primary reason most paranormal investigations take place at night is to minimize outside contamination of the investigation site. The amount of noise that is generated by normal activities during daylight hours may surprise you when reviewing audio recordings.*

6

TOOLS OF THE TRADE

When it comes to paranormal research, there are a wide range of tools a paranormal investigator can choose from to assist them. Some are as simple and inexpensive as paper and pencil, while others are technological marvels costing thousands of dollars. Let's discuss some of these in more detail and learn how, when properly used, they can aid in a paranormal investigation. We will study the following:

Notebook
Digital Audio Recorder
Digital Photograph Camera
Field Meters
Thermometers (surface and ambient)
Video Camera
    Hand Held Infrared Cameras
    Closed Circuit Infrared Cameras
    Full and Dual Spectrum Cameras
    Thermal Imaging Camera
Other Devices
    Motion Sensors
    Data Loggers
Controversial Devices
    The Ovilus
    The Frank's Box

TOOLS OF THE TRADE

Notebooks

One of the most important tools that every investigator should have is also the cheapest. A notebook and a pencil are without a doubt one of the most valuable tools a paranormal investigator can have in their possession during an investigation. Keeping a notebook and pencil with you at all times not only allows you to document the claims in regards to paranormal activity related to a case, it also allows you to log your own thoughts and notes by keeping a running journal of the events that occur during the investigation. When leaving an investigation there is no doubt that you will feel energized and find it easy to remember just about every detail of what you experienced. However, those memories tend to fade quickly and before you know it you will find yourself questioning the order of specific events. It is easy to see just how counter productive this can be when trying to prove or disprove claims of paranormal activity. This is where the notebook really pays off provided you faithfully log all events in the notebook as they happen. By doing so, the events of the evening will be there for you when you want to validate finds or review potential evidence that may have been captured. The notebook is quite simply the foundation for all of your other equipment and tools, so keep it with you always and use it often.

Digital Audio Recorder

A digital audio recorder is a recording device, typically small enough to fit into a shirt pocket, with at least one microphone on it designed to capture audio recordings. They have been used professionally in the business world for decades to record notes and dictation by capturing the audio they pickup and storing it to internal memory.

Using a digital recorder as opposed to an analog based model has several advantages; it is much quicker to locate specific areas in the audio recording during review, as well as making it easier to move the audio from the recorder to a computer for deeper analysis. Tape based recorders require the purchase of tapes and given the fact that as paranormal researchers we never reuse any type of magnetic media, this forces us to purchase new tapes for each investigation and that quickly becomes expensive and cumbersome. The reason we do not reuse tapes is due to the nature of magnetic tape itself, once used, you can never be certain that previous recordings have been completely overwritten. The possibility that there may be residual data on a tape from a previous recording session lessens the integrity of any evidence captured and stored to a previously used tape media.

Figure 1.6 Olympus Model WS-110 Digital Audio Recorder

TOOLS OF THE TRADE

Digital audio recorders satisfy three critical investigation needs:

- They capture what you and the people around you are doing during the investigation. This works well to supplement the journal you keep and can assist in logging what happened and when it happened on an investigation.

- They can capture other external sounds; things such as audible disembodied sounds, animal sounds, footsteps, knocking, and more.

- Digital audio recorders are excellent at capturing electronic voice phenomena during investigations.

A disembodied sound refers to anything you audibly hear during an investigation that seems to come from no where or no one in particular. Some examples of disembodied sounds are voices, footsteps, and unexplained banging. When a digital audio recorder captures disembodied sounds that are audibly heard during an investigation it helps to validate that experience and gives the investigator some solid evidence to log for that case.

Electronic Voice Phenomena, or EVP for short, are the polar opposite of disembodied sounds and is a term used to describe any recordings of voices or sounds that were not audibly heard during an investigation and have no natural explanation. EVPs range in classification based on quality, as discussed in chapter three. Capturing a sound or voice which was not audibly heard or easily explained by natural events during an investigation is an extremely valuable piece of evidence. EVPs can often provide you deeper insight into the type of paranormal activity occurring in that location.

Digital Photograph Camera

Digital cameras are a very valuable tool as they serve well to visually document a location. Often when reviewing information and data captured during an investigation, or when reviewing journal entries and notes, it can become important to confirm information about the physical layout of the environment. Digital cameras provide a means to record this information in the form of photographs that can be reviewed as often as needed.

In addition to photographing a location for documentation purposes, digital cameras have been known to also capture paranormal activity. While one must be careful not to confuse glare, flash effects, lighting flares, or similar natural anomalies associated with photography as paranormal evidence, digital cameras can be used to capture things visually that are often unseen at the time the photograph was taken. Many people also believe paranormal energy sources can be captured and documented utilizing this tool.

The nature of the digital photography camera, much like the digital audio recorder, makes it very easy to transfer the images captured to a computer for analysis and reporting.

Field Meters

There are a number of meters available that can be used in the realm of paranormal research in order to monitor the states of energy fields in a given area. The two primary fields we tend to focus on are electric and magnetic, combined electromagnetic.

TOOLS OF THE TRADE

The World Health Organization defines the fields as follows:

> **"Electric fields** are created by differences in voltage: the higher the voltage, the stronger will be the resultant field."

> **"Magnetic fields** are created when electric current flows: the greater the current, the stronger the magnetic field. An electric field will exist even when there is no current flowing. If current does flow, the strength of the magnetic field will vary with power consumption but the electric field strength will be constant."

Many things in our environment create electromagnetic fields. There is a theory related to EMF fields which suggests that paranormal entities may either generate or have the ability to alter electromagnetic fields. In an effort to observe and document this in an attempt to validate this theory, paranormal investigators use electromagnetic field meters, which are more commonly referred to as EMF meters.

There are many types of EMF meters available on the market and while all essentially monitor the same thing, they often go about it using completely different methods. It would be difficult to list all of the manufacturers and brands here while attempting to elaborate on how they sense EMF fields. There are however, two distinct differences to note regarding types of meters available. There are meters that read and display EMF fields in their proximity and continue to register and display those readings as they change, as well as meters that only detect and display fluctuations. The meters designed to detect fluctuations have the ability to self-zero or normalize and only respond to changes in the field. For example, if a device were switched on that produced a constant electromagnetic field; the first type of meter would register that field as being detected and the strength of the field would be constantly displayed. The second type of meter would register that field as being detected and then gradually self-zero or normalize provided the field is stable, and only register and display readings if that field changed again.

Both types of meters are excellent tools. A meter that gives a constant reading is useful for both detecting EMF anomalies as well as taking base readings of an area to look for naturally occurring EMF sources such as wiring. A self-zeroing meter is an excellent tool for detecting sudden changes in the EMF in a given area. These changes can be recorded to correlate with other evidence of paranormal activity.

Before making the decision to utilize an EMF meter during your investigation, we strongly recommend that you carefully study the technical specifications as well as the operating instructions of any meter you intend to use prior to employing it in the field.

Thermometers

There are two types of thermometers we want to discuss: those designed to read ambient air temperature, and those designed to read surface temperature. Both types are used in paranormal investigations but it is essential to understand that they serve two very different roles.

Surface temperature thermometers typically use an infrared sensor to determine the temperature of the surface of an object. They use an infrared beam to sample the area of a surface in order to calculate the temperature of that surface. It is important to understand that the further away you are from the surface being measured the larger the sample area will be.

TOOLS OF THE TRADE

The ambient temperature thermometers alternatively are designed and intended to read and display the temperature of the surrounding air in a given area. Traditional analog thermometers can be used, but digital models are much more reactive and can give more exact readings. Digital ambient thermometers are often paired with other investigation equipment such as EMF meters, and are an excellent tool for gathering evidence of temperature drops or spikes in a given location during an investigation.

Video Cameras

Video cameras are one of the best yet most expensive tools that an investigator can utilize during an investigation. They range in type as well as use and can be leveraged for everything from documenting the activities of the investigation team, monitoring other equipment being used to detect a paranormal event, and even capturing paranormal activity directly.

Before we discuss the different types of cameras and how they are used in this field, let's talk about some of the important things we should keep in mind that apply to all cameras regardless of their purpose. All cameras should be capable of recording in digital format as well as have a means of transferring the captured video to a computer for analysis. When possible it is best to use a camera which stores the data on digital media, such as hard drives or memory cards. Tape based video cameras should be a last resort since purchasing new tapes for each investigation can become very expensive given the fact that no tape media should ever be used more than one time.

Handheld Digital Video Cameras

The handheld digital video camera is one of the most common video cameras used during a paranormal investigation. The camera must have the ability to record images utilizing an infrared light source thereby allowing the camera to "see" in the dark. Cameras of this nature have a built-in function that essentially removes the infrared filter that most cameras have in order to record images in zero light. This is essential for recording in all situations. Handheld cameras should also have the ability to be mounted on a tripod and, as mentioned above, it is best to use a camera that stores its video to a hard drive or memory card. This eliminates the need to swap tapes during an investigation and it saves on the cost associated with buying new tapes. Extra batteries for the camera are also strongly recommended as most cameras will only operate on a single charge for approximately 3 – 4 hours.

Handheld digital cameras can be used for a variety of purposes. They serve well to record paranormal events because they are portable and travel with you during the investigation. They can also be tripod mounted to record an area of suspected activity even while you are not present. In addition to being used to capture evidence of paranormal activity, handheld cameras are excellent tools for simply documenting the events of the investigation itself, similar to using audio recorders to track investigators and the events of the investigation. It can be incredibly valuable to review video footage recorded by the handheld camera as a means to validate other evidence during the review process.

TOOLS OF THE TRADE

Closed Circuit Video Cameras

Closed circuit video cameras, also referred to as CCTV cameras, are stationary cameras which are hardwired back to a central recording device and are commonly used by most paranormal investigators. Cameras of this type must have infrared capabilities if filming at night. This means not only should the camera be able to detect infrared light but there should also be a source of infrared light. These are often imbedded in the camera but external infrared illuminators can be used if needed.

The closed circuit cameras should be placed in areas of known or suspected activity or any area you need to monitor in an attempt to debunk suspected activity. Cameras of this nature should utilize a dedicated cable to send the video images back to a centralized recording device, such as a computer with a video capture card or a dedicated DVR security system. It is highly recommended to steer clear of systems that use wireless technology to send video images back to the recorder as these systems are susceptible to electronic interference which renders any evidence captured by them questionable.

While these cameras don't usually include sound they are the heart of capturing visual evidence. Like the handheld camera, they too can be used to help in the evidence review process as they typically record during the entire investigation.

Thermal Imaging Camera

Quite possibly one of the most coveted devices which are also professed by many investigators to be the "Holy Grail" of paranormal research tools, is the thermal imaging camera. These cameras are designed to render video images based on the surface temperature of objects in their focal path. The images are rendered using a predefined pallet of colors which corresponds to the surface temperature of objects relative to each other. While they are not good for general filming of an investigation, they are excellent for capturing temperature anomalies such as cold spots.

Not all thermal imaging cameras are capable of recording video and the ones that do often require an external storage solution. While all cameras of this nature are capable of recording still thermal images, utilizing a camera which is capable of capturing video is essential and produces more compelling evidence. We highly recommend using a thermal imaging camera in tandem with a standard infrared camera as well as having a voice recorder running. As stated earlier, thermal imaging cameras render video images based on the surface temperature of objects in its focal path but they are also susceptible to detecting reflected heat as well. Should you detect a temperature anomaly during the review process, it is essential that you are able to refer to footage from a standard infrared camera that was used in parallel with the thermal camera to determine if the anomaly recorded is in fact a reflection from another heat source.

It is extremely important to carefully document the whereabouts of all of your investigators during the investigation while using a thermal imaging camera. A person walking across an area, or sitting in a chair or on a bed can leave a lasting thermal imprint that may take time to dissipate depending on environmental conditions. Even a hand placed causally on a wall can leave a temperature signature that will last for several minutes. You want to be completely sure that any evidenced captured is genuine and not simply a by-product of one of your investigators.

There are two things of importance to note regarding the use of thermal imaging cameras during paranormal research. First, they are excellent tools for use in outside investigations as they help overcome some of the challenges associated with this type of investigation. Often in the dark, noises are heard or movement is detected and without being able to clearly see the cause those noises may be misleading. Thermal imaging cameras serve not only as a tool to capture paranormal evidence, but in this case can quickly detect the presence of an animal or person that may be causing the disturbance. Second, you should be aware that thermal imaging cameras only detect surface temperature and do not have the ability to detect ambient temperature. The reason this is particularly important to those of us employing this device for paranormal research is there has been some discussion pertaining to this device's ability to "see" an entity given the fact that they are not generally considered a "solid" mass. While there is some evidence depicting the presence of a human form captured with this type of device circulating out there, this device is not supposed to be able to record such an anomaly. Given the fact that we do not really know any details related to an entity's ability to take form, more research is needed before forming an opinion or theory.

Full and Dual Spectrum Cameras

The electromagnetic spectrum is the range of all possible frequencies of electromagnetic radiation (see Figure 1.7). Included in this spectrum is visible light which most humans are easily able to perceive. The goal of any "spectrum" cameras is to capture specific frequencies of the electromagnetic radiation range and convert it to visible light.

While full spectrum typically refers to the camera's ability to capture anything in the infrared, visible, and ultraviolet light range, dual spectrum cameras typically block visible light and capture only infrared and ultraviolet light.

Although these cameras were originally developed for industrial applications, recent experiments in the field of paranormal research have produced compelling evidence which has led to the increased use of cameras capable of "seeing" ultraviolet light. Using a dual or full spectrum camera gives the added benefit of visually seeing and recording images in these other frequency ranges that our eyes are not capable of seeing.

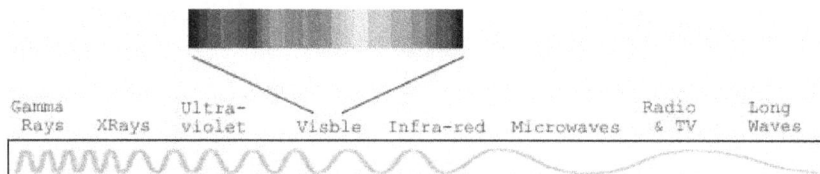

Figure 1.7 Illustration of the Electromagnetic Spectrum

Motion Sensors

Motion sensors are devices that are used to sense motion and are used during paranormal research in several ways. Motion sensors can be used as standalone devices that simply alert you when something passes through an area via an audible or visible alarm. They can also be linked to infrared photo cameras that take photographs when motion is detected via the sensor. Some motion sensors work by producing a field or light source around them, often as an infrared beam or laser. Breaking the beam or entering the field triggers the alarm. Other motion sensors work by detecting vibration which triggers the alarm. When using motion sensors that detect vibration, great care needs to be taken as these can react to your own investigators walking around a location.

Data Loggers

Data loggers are devices that are designed to remain stationary at a particular location and continuously take sensor readings while recording them to either internal storage or sending them back to a computer for processing.

Data loggers are available in a number of configurations depending on the type of sensors that are attached or built into them. Some of the key sensors to look for center on what we've already talked about, such as temperature, electromagnetic field changes, humidity, and sound.

Data loggers are extremely valuable tools for recording the conditions of an area over an extended period of time. In our experience it is important to include an audio recorder as well as a video camera in the same location as the data logger. This allows you to correlate any recorded anomalies from the data logger with what was happening in the room at the time of the anomaly. At the very least, place an audio recorder with the data logger as it is essential in helping to validate anything captured by the data logger.

Other Devices

Up to this point we have discussed a number of different types of equipment ranging from the simple notepad to cameras capable of capturing things we can't see with the naked eye. Each of the tools we have discussed to this point is what we would consider valid and worthy tools of the trade, some of them being essential to conducting a solid scientific based investigation. They have a proven history of use and are capable of producing solid results. They can be used to capture events of an investigation ranging from tracking the movement of the investigators themselves, to the potential of recording paranormal activity. The baseline of data that can be captured by these devices is well established and when an anomaly occurs it is usually noticeable.

In this section we're going to talk about two other tools that have been used in the course of paranormal investigation. These tools are less common or less "provable" in their results and considered highly controversial by most in the field. We are not attempting to discredit them in anyway, but are merely pointing out that the science behind them or the nature of these tools is, to a degree, something to be studied in itself. These are by no means the only controversial tools used by investigators, but they are among the more well known having been made popular by several paranormal based television shows.

The Ovilus

The Ovilus is an interesting tool to say the least and was introduced to the paranormal field by a company entitled Digital Dousing. It should be noted as of this writing Digital Dousing no longer offers the Ovilus for sale as they have stopped production.

The device had a number of operational modes but its basic function was to use readings obtained from sensors built into the unit and translate those readings into words or phonetic sounds that the user of the device could audibly here. The general premise behind the device was to allow spirits to manipulate the fields around the device thus causing the device to speak for them.

The use of this device is considered highly controversial among scientific based investigators due to the potential randomness of its responses and the lack of verifiable evidence that spirits are actually controlling the device.

The Frank's Box or Ghost Box

The Frank's Box, named after its original creator Frank Sumption, was originally created in an attempt to provide a means to communicate with the dead. The device scans radio frequencies in the AM and FM bands constantly creating white noise. Several theories suggest that white noise makes it easier for a spirit or entity to form words when attempting to communicate during EVP sessions.

While there are now numerous devices available being sold under different names this type of device is now more commonly referred to as a ghost box. This type of device is used in a similar fashion to the Ovilus and is another piece of electronic equipment aimed at communication with the spirit world. Like the Ovilus, it is considered a highly controversial piece of equipment because of its random nature and lack of re-enforceable evidence that something like this can do what it claims.

Summary

While there are countless manufacturers marketing numourous types of equipment for use in the paranormal field. You are responcible for knowing how to use each piece of equipment as well as its limitations. The time must be invested to research each piece of equipment you choose to employ during your investigations to make sure they function as expected and do what they claim.

7

GENERAL STANDARDS

There is no doubt about it, investigating the paranormal can be fun, challenging, and exciting. However, we should not lose sight of the fact that it can also be dangerous and problematic. This chapter is intended to introduce you to a set of core rules that are accepted by majority of investigators in the paranormal field and are adhered to while conducting investigations. The rules are intended to help establish a safe environment for everyone involved as well as reduce the potential of creating false positives during the process of gathering evidence.

Know the Environment

Regardless of whether you are entering a home to look for spirits or tracking the latest Bigfoot sighting, it is important to become familiar with the surroundings as well as the challenges and dangers they may present. If you are entering an old building you should be aware that the floors may be rotted and unstable, ceilings have the potential of collapsing, and also be aware that asbestos may be present at that location. Even if you are simply investigating a client's home it is a good idea to study what goes on in and around the dwelling. If your investigation is outdoors in the dark, take the time to visit the location during the day to document the terrain as well as what animal life inhabits the area. Look for things such as cliffs, sink holes, and fallen debris that may pose a danger to you and your team members.

Never Investigate Alone

This rule is important for several reasons. First, there are safety concerns. If something happens to you, you need to rely on your partner to get you help. Always let others who are not part of the investigation know your exact whereabouts and when you plan on returning. This is very important in the event that something happens to your entire team. Second, if you do experience anything paranormal there are two of you to witness it. Honor the buddy system; always have at least two investigators at a location during an active investigation and never approach an investigation alone.

Respect your Client's Claims

While you may approach your investigations scientifically, you must keep in mind that many people have strong religious beliefs or believe in spirits they feel they are sensitive to. There are occasions when people develop extreme theories as to what they may be experiencing. Often these individuals have spoken to others who may have misguided them resulting in a mix of ideas regarding what they are experiencing. At times it is hard to listen to these theories with sincerity, but we have to keep in mind that these events are very real for the people who are experiencing them. The events may be traumatizing for them and they often believe with passion that they are being harassed by some unseen force. It is important that you look beyond that and conduct a thorough scientific investigation while respecting your client's beliefs as well.

Do Not Make False Claims

Do not make claims to your clients that you are able to rid them of their paranormal problems. While it is possible to debunk all claims of activity by finding natural explanations for the causes, it is rare. Sometimes you'll find no evidence. Don't give your client false hope that you can rid them of their torments. Your job is to try to validate their experiences by capturing valid evidence, not performing an exorcism for them. Leave the act of exorcism to the Church as they are the experts.

Never Trespass

Trespassing on private property is the quickest way to compromise your integrity as an investigator, and it will get you in trouble with the authorities if you are caught. If someone is willing to break the law in order to conduct an investigation then one has to question the rest of their character when it comes to the evidence they present. It is important to respect the privacy of property and land owners as well as their reasons for preventing access. In some cases locations may be off limits for safety reasons. In others the owner may wish to keep paranormal events private. There are plenty of locations with alleged paranormal events out there to investigate, but you must always get permission to enter a location prior to conducting an investigation.

Get It in Writing

It is strongly recommended you use a simple permission form signed by your clients which grants permission to your team prior to the investigation. The form should basically document why you are there, list the members of your party, and state that you have the location owners' permission to be there. This form must be signed by the owner and is extremely important if the police are called by concerned neighbors.

Follow your Gut Instinct

There will be times when you are contacted by a potential client to do an investigation and something does not feel right about the case. That *"something"* can be your concerns about the location of the supposed activity, the mental state of the client, or the activity reported is beyond your ability to handle. Regardless of the reason, there is no shame in turning down an investigative opportunity if it does not feel right.

Establish Boundaries

Talk to your client about what they are comfortable with regarding the investigation. As simple as this sounds, ask the client if there are any locations where members of your team should not go. Keep in mind, especially at residential locations; you and your team are investigating the living spaces of your clients. Make sure they know it is okay to set areas as off limits, and that you will respect their wishes.

GENERAL STANDARDS

Be Professional

The actions of your team members reflect the integrity and character of your group. Always conduct your investigations in a professional manner and address all situations professionally. Do not use foul language, violate established boundaries, or go through a client's personal effects (drawers, boxes, etc.). Be respectful of their property and their beliefs. Do not try to indoctrinate them into your belief system.

Communicate

While you should not rely on a cell phone during an investigation it is advisable to have one with you in the event you require emergency services. Make use of two-way radios to communicate with team members but make them aware that these devices have the potential of producing false positives on your equipment.

Carry Photo ID

All members of your team must carry some form of photo identification. The authorities tend to get very irritable if you can not prove to them that you are who you say you are. In the event you or a member of your team becomes disoriented and gets lost, the identification will assist the authorities in helping them make it home.

Be Aware of Medical Situations

It is advisable to make a first aid kit part of your standard equipment. You should also know about any medical condition a member of your group has that could pose a health risk to them during an investigation. If they have a history of breathing or heart problems which could be life threatening, having this information could save their life in the event a medical situation occurs. You should also be aware of any allergies your investigators may have, specifically allergies to insects such as bee. It is recommended that you and your team be trained in basic first aid including how to treat allergic reactions, snake bites, and similar ailments.

Never Smoke During an Investigation

Smoking in general during an investigation is questionable, but never smoke while conducting an active investigation. Respect your client's property as well as their wishes. If you do smoke, do it outside in a designated area away from the investigation. Tobacco smoke has been linked to misleading evidence in photographs and on video recordings.

Remove or Secure Camera Straps and Lens Covers

Before using a camera or video camera to record images ensure the strap and lens covers are secure. You want to ensure that neither of these items obstruct or interfere with the images you capture. Failure to do this could compromise the integrity of visual evidence.

GENERAL STANDARDS

Secure Long Hair

Individuals with long hair must secure their hair as it does pose a risk of getting caught in or on something during an investigation. Also, long hair has the potential of creating false anomalies while photographing or video recording.

Use Small Investigation Teams

As stated earlier, you should never investigate alone. However, you should also keep your investigation teams small as it is difficult to keep track of the actions of large teams during an active investigation. A simple thing like moving around in a room needs to be documented to prevent false positives when reviewing evidence, specifically audio recordings. With larger groups it can be extremely challenging to note all of this activity. As a result we recommend breaking your team down into smaller groups of no more than three or four individuals when sending them into a given location during an investigation.

Always Use Fresh Batteries

All equipment needs to be in proper operating condition when conducting an investigation. One of the leading causes of equipment malfunction is weak or dead batteries. Make sure you always start an investigation with fresh batteries to ensure the integrity of your equipment. One thing that will quickly become apparent is the amount of money your team spends on single use batteries. You may want to consider investing in rechargeable batteries. Although the initial investment is hard to justify in the beginning, the long term savings will be worth it.

Never Whisper During an Investigation

For some reason investigators tend to whisper during an investigation. If something needs to be said it is better to speak at normal levels as whispering can be difficult to distinguish from legitimate audio anomalies. Encourage your team to speak at normal levels to make their voices easy to distinguish during the evidence review process.

Never Run

We will be the first to admit that it is human nature to run when confronted by something that frightens you. However, running poses the single greatest risk of injury to everyone involved in an investigation, not to mention is the single most unprofessional thing you can do. If the client sees a paranormal investigator running from their property out of fear from an occurrence, we cannot expect them to accept and deal rationally with any possible future paranormal activity. It is imperative to remain calm and confident.

Summary

We have just covered what the majority of investigators in the paranormal field consider to be the core list of rules each team should follow. The fact is, each paranormal group should have their own set of rules, which may or may not contain all of the rules in our list. The important thing is you need rules in place in order to maintain some sense of order and safety during an investigation.

8

PERFORMING A SOUND
INVESTIGATION

Now that you have a better understanding of just how broad a subject the supernatural realm really is, let's discuss some of the many challenges that paranormal researchers are faced with regarding documenting conclusive evidence during their investigations.

There are countless theories related to the study of the paranormal and the supernatural. There are just as many techniques and methods that teams and individuals employ during an investigation in an attempt to document and prove the claims of the paranormal. In addition to the many honest people trying to study the phenomena, we cannot deny that there are also those out there who fabricate fraudulent evidence and hoaxes. The actions of these few misguided individuals result in a feeding frenzy for the skeptics, making the task of having legitimate findings taken seriously almost insurmountable.

The Challenges

With the countless obstacles each of us in this field face, how does one attempt to successfully document claims of the paranormal? What compels people to get involved in a field teeming with so much controversy? The simple answer to these questions is that far too many people the world over have experienced or witnessed first hand phenomena that simply cannot be explained. This raises another question: if the phenomena happens so often and is witnessed by so many different people in locations all over the world, why is it so hard for us to document the phenomena or at the very least prove the existence of the phenomena itself?

Documenting sound, verifiable proof of the paranormal is the goal for anyone seriously involved in this field of study. With a little analysis and a strong, solid set of procedures we aim to show you how to approach investigating and documenting claims of the paranormal while mitigating controversy.

Before we delve into anything procedural we need to review a few basics. We covered the definition of the term paranormal earlier, but let's take a quick look at the very basic definition of the term, which literally means beyond normal. While we admit some of the topics that comprise this field are incredible and difficult to grasp, we must keep in mind that we are simply dealing with topics that are considered to be beyond normal. To help you put this in to perspective, consider the fact that not all that long ago the mysteries of everyday things such as electricity and electromagnetic radiation were considered beyond normal understanding. Scientific study and investigation is what lead us to develop an understanding of electricity and electromagnetic radiation. In order to approach and study paranormal events scientifically, several things must be kept in mind:

1. The study of anything involves observation and these observations can be done with the naked eye as well as equipment designed to more closely study the subject matter.

2. When investigating the paranormal it is important that we remain open minded when studying events directly observed. We must also work to develop ways to observe and record events indirectly through the use of accepted methods and equipment.

3. Equipment used should have a well established history of performance, meaning its functions should be well understood and the outcome of those functions should be well established in various environments.

For example, we know that thermometers display temperature and EMF meters have a proven ability to detect electromagnetic fields. These devices are scientifically accepted, have a valid use and demonstratable science behind their operation and functionality. At the opposite end of the spectrum, attempting to use people with proclaimed psychic abilities is not accepted by the scientific community. We must remember, these abilities are considered paranormal anomalies themselves and we cannot validate the paranormal by using the paranormal. We are not suggesting in any way that these abilities do not exist or that the individuals who claim to have them are lying. We highly encourage the study of these special abilities, but what these individuals see, hear, or feel cannot be used to prove paranormal phenomena because they are considered part of the phenomena.

The Scientific Method

In order to have our findings considered credible scientifically we must conduct our investigations using the scientific method. The scientific method is defined as follows:

"Scientific method refers to a body of techniques for investigating phenomena, acquiring new knowledge, or correcting and integrating previous knowledge. To be termed scientific, a method of inquiry must be based on gathering observable, empirical and measurable evidence subject to specific principles of reasoning. A scientific method consists of the collection of data through observation and experimentation, and the formulation and testing of hypotheses." - Merriam-Webster

We also need to become familiar with the following two terms which will be beneficial as we proceed through this chapter:

Empirical – denotes information gained by means of observation, experience, or experiment.

Reasoning – is the process of forming conclusions, judgments, or inferences from facts or premises.

To summarize, in order to approach anything with the scientific method we need to be able to observe it and measure it as well as apply a principle of reasoning. One such model of the scientific method, which is employed during our investigations, works like this:

1. Build a body of information on a subject based on current knowledge, experience, and evidence.

2. Form a conjecture or theory based on that knowledge.

3. Test that theory by experimentation and observation of evidence.

4. Prove the theory correct with solid evidence and logical conclusions, or refine the theory and test again.

So far everything seems to make sense from a scientific approach as we now have an understanding of the scientific method as well as a model to follow which is reasonable and logical. However there is one glaring problem; we need observable and measurable evidence. How can we observe and measure, with any accuracy, something that we cannot see or touch with any reliability? The answer is correlated evidence. Our best method to record credible evidence in the paranormal field of study is to attempt to correlate our findings. In chapter six we detailed many of the tools used during a typical paranormal investigation, all of which have the potential of providing us with a solid body of evidence. Utilizing the scientific method and attempting to link our findings as we just discussed will give us our best chance of proving many of the paranormal claims we study.

Imagine, for example, that you were performing an investigation and you hear a disembodied voice. This is one piece of evidence and at best would be considered a personal experience.

This piece of evidence is however easy to dispute because there is nothing tangible to back up your claim. Now, suppose you were able to capture the same voice on a digital audio recorder located in the room with you. You now have a tangible piece of evidence to back up your claim. The problem with this particular piece of evidence is that it may be easily refuted as an internal or external audio source. But what if you are able to add to this simple disembodied voice, which was captured on a digital audio recorder, a range of other evidence from multiple types of equipment used during that same investigation?

Envision for a moment you had cameras stationed in the room, as well as the adjoining rooms to where the voice was captured. These cameras can help prove that the voice was not associated with anyone inside that location. Also imagine you were able to capture a temperature drop on a data logger as well as an EMF spike at the exact moment the disembodied voice is recorded. You would end up with multiple pieces of evidence which all happened at the exact time the EVP was captured. This is the process of correlation and it gives you solid, observable proof that something happened and was recorded. Figure 1.8 illustrates the principle we are talking about. If we are able to repeat these steps every time, over time we should be able to recognize patterns in the data which should validate our theories.

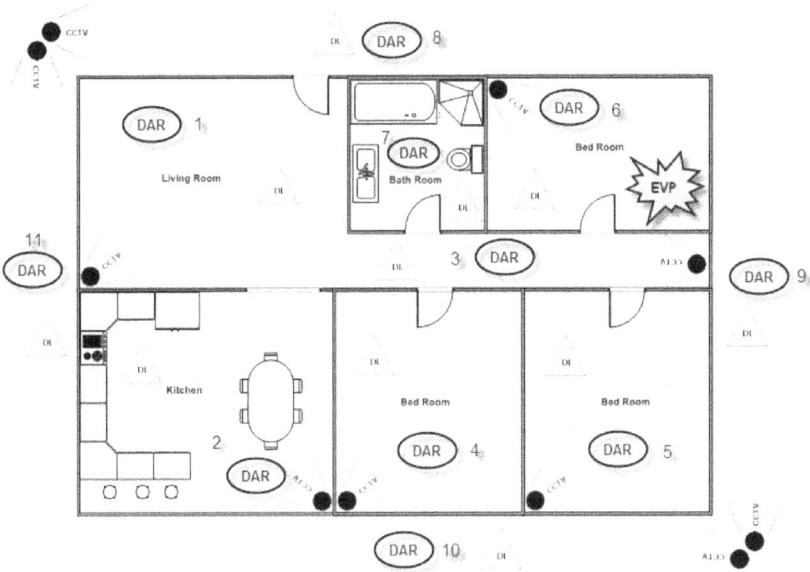

Figure 1.8 Scientific Method – Correlation

Using the technique of correlating evidence and eliminating normal and natural causes related to claims of paranormal activity will give us the material we need to begin forming logical theories regarding this field. With enough evidence, experience, and experimentation, sound scientific theories can be formed.

Investigation Techniques and Procedures

In this next section we will detail the investigation techniques and procedures that we have developed and use on each investigation our paranormal research group conducts. While there is always room for improvement and refinement, we developed these standards with the intention of providing consistency as well as an attempt to mitigate points of contention while gathering evidence during an investigation.

83

You will see as you read through the procedures that they are very structured, thorough, and repetitive. Some of the steps documented may seem obvious but you would be surprised just how easy it is to stray from these steps if you are not careful. The goal of these procedures is to provide a method for obtaining solid, recordable evidence by consistently documenting all accounts of an investigation. By doing so we minimize any doubt from the evidence obtained. This is accomplished by having all investigators function as a team, providing a system where everyone performs each task the same way, and making them aware of the claims before the investigation begins. A team that is well prepared prior to the investigation will perform with greater consistency during the investigation.

The following list of terms is used throughout the procedures. While most terms are self explanatory, we felt it would be beneficial to take a moment to define them as they pertain to the procedures we are about to cover.

- **Recordings** – refers to audio and video recordings.
- **Active Investigation** – refers to investigating an area actively with investigators present in that area.
- **Passive Investigation** – refers to investigating an area without investigators present using cameras and/or audio recording devices.
- **Static Audio Recorder** – refers to a stationary voice recorder setup in a location and left to run during the entire investigation.
- **HQ** – base of operations where team will meet. This is also the location of the DVR system, monitor, equipment storage, etc.

> **Investigation Journal** – log book used to maintain a record of all events that occur during the investigation such as area information, equipment location, investigation team movement, and experiences.

> **Personal Investigation Journal** – log book that each investigator records their personal experiences in during the investigation. Information in these logs should not shared during the investigation. These logs must be turned in to the case manager at the end of the investigation.

Our investigations are structured in four stages. These stages help us manage each phase of the investigation and ensure consistency. The four phases of an investigation are; Pre-Investigation, Setup, Execution, and Close.

>>> Pre-Investigation Phase <<<

The pre-investigation steps must be completed prior to showing up at a location to conduct the investigation.

1.0 **Conduct interview with client and place emphasis on documenting the following:**
   1. Reported claims and types of phenomena being experienced.
   2. Areas in which activity has been experienced.
   3. Names of individuals who have personally witnessed claims.
   4. Pertinent information related to everyone occupying the location in question.

Note! | *The use of an investigation interview form is highly recommended as it will help you standardize the questions you ask and ensure the data collected is consistent and thorough.*

1.1 **Scheduling Investigation with client:**
   1. Establish date of investigation with client.
   2. Establish start time of investigation with client.
   3. Acquire all contact information from client.

Note!

Using a team based calendar where everyone is able to update their availability will minimize scheduling issues for your team's case manager. The goal is to schedule the investigation with the client once at the time of initial contact. Try to avoid delays by going back and forth with the client as this tends to indicate that your group is un-organized and sets a bad first impression.

1.2 **Prepare required forms needed for investigation:**

1. Waiver and Release from Liability Form – this form releases the client or property owner from any liability which may result from injury or damage to your equipment that could occur during an investigation.
2. Permission to Investigate Form – this form grants permission to your team to investigate a location in the event you are questioned by local authorities.
3. Confidentiality Agreement Form – this form states that you and all members of your team agree to keep all details of the case confidential.
4. Identify team members that will be involved with the investigation and confirm participation.

1.3 **Meet with team members to discuss the following:**

1. Claims.
2. History of location.
3. People involved.
4. Impact or affect the activity is having on the occupants.
5. Equipment needs for investigation.
6. Travel plans if necessary.
   6.1 Mode of transportation.
   6.2 Lodging.

>>> Set-up Phase <<<

2.0 Meet with client:
1. Introduce team.
2. Discuss any new developments.
3. Take a tour of the location focusing on critical points of activity or areas crucial to the location.
4. Collect pertinent information related to everyone occupying the location in question.
5. Establish boundaries of investigation.
6. Have all on-site forms signed by location owner.
7. Answer any questions from residence owner.
8. Take base readings and document site plan or building floor plan.
9. Document the status of lights, doors, windows, heating and air conditioning systems so they can be returned to their original state at the conclusion of the investigation should the need arise to turn anything off.
10. Document anything that may impact the investigation (broken windows, dripping faucets, etc.).

2.1 Team Meeting:
1. Have all team members turn off their cell phones as they are known to interfere with equipment such as EMF meters and can introduce noise contamination during the investigation.
2. Review the following:
    2.1 Claims.
    2.2 History of location.
    2.3 People involved in activity.
    2.4 Impact or affect the activity is having on the occupants.
    2.5 Equipment needs for investigation.
3. Discuss Primary Objectives:
    3.1 Define the rooms or areas at the location that will be investigated.
    3.2 Equipment that will be used and its location.
    3.3 Investigation techniques that should or should not be utilized during the investigation.
    3.4 Anything else that is critical to the initial plan or the investigation.

4. Devise equipment placement plan based on site tour, team observations, and any new information obtained during your discussion with the client in step one. Your plan should include:

    4.1 Areas identified for active investigation.

    4.2 Equipment to be used.

    4.3 Areas identified for passive investigation.

    4.4 Equipment to be used and the location for placement.

5. Bring all equipment into location.

6. Establish location of HQ. It is our opinion that the location of HQ should always remain outside of the area being investigated when possible. This will minimize any chances of contaminating any evidence captured during the investigation.

    6.1 Setup HQ.

    6.2 Setup CCTV DVR, monitors, communications, and start investigation journal.

2.2 Equipment Placement:

1. Run any audio and video cabling that may be needed. It is important to secure all cables to minimize any chance of injury. Standard duct tape works well for this purpose.

2. Setup static cameras, infrared illuminators and audio recorders in locations as identified in the placement plan.

    2.1 Update investigation journal with equipment location and the name of the team member who was responsible for setting it up.

3. Setup data loggers, stationary EMF meters, stationary sound level meters, and vibration detection devices.

    3.1 Update investigation journal with equipment location and the name of the team member who was responsible for setting it up.

4. Perform full base reading sweep of location. Base readings should be taken inside as well as outside and should include the following information:

    4.1 Temperature

    4.2 EMF

    4.3 Still photographs

    4.4 Notes related to observations that may impact the investigation such as squeaky floor boards or doors, mechanical noises, loose or broken fixtures, outside noises or sounds that may be captured during EVP sessions, ect...

PERFORMING A SOUND INVESTIGATION

It may be helpful to record the baseline sweep on a hand held audio recorder or record the entire process on video. We found this extra step can be beneficial in several ways. If an object has moved at some point during the evening you can use the video recorded during the baseline sweep as confirmation.

Note!

2.3 **Guidelines for Portable Equipment Use:**
1. Document what equipment will be used during the investigation of a location in the investigation journal.
    1.1 At least one audio recorder is mandatory.
    1.2 Room investigation log is mandatory.
    1.3 Standard EMF meter is mandatory.
    1.4 Video camera is mandatory.
         This requirement can be fulfilled with a stationary CCTV Camera.

TriField EMF Meters
1. Place on a non-static inducing surface and turn the unit on.
2. Adjust volume.
3. Allow it to normalize.

K-II EMF Meters
1. Place on a non-static inducing surface and turn it on.
2. Verify that there are no constant readings on the K-II meter, if there are try to identify possible sources for the readings.
3. If the need to isolate an EMF source arises the K-II meter is the preferred method of verification as this meter is less susceptible to false readings when moved.

Standard EMF meters
1. Place on a non-static inducing surface and power on.
2. Allow it to stabilize.
3. Activate record mode on the meter if the option is present.

Video Cameras:
1. Use tripods if possible.
2. Setup portable cameras to capture the investigation and any spots of notable activity.
    2.1 If necessary configure cameras to record other equipment such as EMF meters or K-II meters.
3. Update personal investigation journal.
    3.1 Note the investigators and equipment in the room in your journal.
    3.2 Confirm base readings such as temperature and EMF.
    3.3 Note the location of each team member in the location.
    3.4 Update the room sketch to include the location of all equipment.

Still Photography

1. Take snapshots with still camera during the investigation.
2. Always verbally announce when you are taking a photo by saying "flash" to give other team members the chance to close their eyes or look away.
3. When taking a photo it is always a good idea to take two shots each time. This will make identifying anomalies much easier during the review process.

2.4 Equipment Verification

1. Verify camera angels.
2. Verify location of all equipment.
3. Ensure CCTV cameras are recording.
4. Start static audio recordings.
5. Turn off all lighting sources.

2.5 Have all team members return to HQ prior to starting the execution phase.

>>> Execution Phase <<<

Note! *The execution phase is the heart of the investigation. This phase should be highly structured and documented. Investigation teams should consist of at least two members but no more than four and all accounts must be documented in the investigation journal.*

3.0 Pre-execution Team Meeting:

1. Take approximately 30 minutes to review the following with your team.
   1.1 Are all members present and accounted for?
   1.2 Are all cell phones powered off?
   1.3 Are all radios functional?
   1.4 Does each member have their investigation journal?
   1.5 Investigation teams are no larger than three members?
   1.6 Define where each team will be investigating and how long each team will occupy the area.
   1.7 All teams must return to HQ prior to investigating another area.
   1.8 Someone must always remain at HQ to monitor equipment and communications. They are also responsible for maintaining the investigation journal.

Note! *The investigation journal is intended to record all aspects of the investigation and as such every detail of the investigation should be documented with date, time, and event.*

3.1 Begin Active Investigation:

1. Investigation Teams
   1.1 Always have at least two investigators in a location during the investigation. This is for safety as well as it allows for confirmation of events.
   1.2 Each investigator is responsible for maintaining their personal investigation journal.
   1.3 Determine if investigators will be sitting, standing or moving around within the location and verbally note that on the audio recorder.
   1.4 All investigators should speak at a normal tone and refrain from whispering during an investigation. This minimizes the possibility of misidentifying the whispers as potential EVPs.

1.5 All active investigations should begin with five to ten minutes of silence. This allows the team to get acclimated to the location as well as take note of any anomalous sounds, lights, etc.

2. After a period of time the team should leave the active investigation area and return to HQ. Teams can be deployed back to that active investigation area or other active investigation areas previous identified.

>>> Close Phase <<<

Note! *During the close phase of the investigation team members should pay close attention to their surroundings to ensure nothing is missed and that everything is in the same order as documented during the setup phase.*

4.0   **Concluding the Investigation:**
1.   Turn on all lights.
2.   Note the readings on any EMF meters with recording capabilities.
3.   Audibly note the date and time the active investigation is ending for each area that contains a static audio recorder prior to ending the recording.
   3.1   Also document this in the investigation journal.
4.   Stop static voice recorder recordings.
5.   Tear down and pack up meters and data loggers.
6.   Stop infrared camera recordings.
7.   Tear down static infrared cameras and audio recorders and stage at HQ.
8.   Tear down audio and video cabling and stage at HQ.
9.   Tear down command center.
10.   Record investigation end time and date in investigation journal.
11.   Load equipment in vehicles.
12.   Reset all lights, doors, HVAC settings, etc. as noted at start of investigation.
13.   Check all rooms and video record close up of location.

Note! *In the past, members of our team have encountered objects that were moved at some point during an investigation but not noticed until the close phase. Due to the fact that we video tape the environment during the set-up phase and document all accounts of the investigation, we were able to determine that these objects were not moved by any of our team members during the investigation and documented the anomaly as potential evidence.*

If the client is still present at the end of the investigation take a moment to meet with them and let them know that you have completed the investigation for the evening. Let them also know that you will need some time to review the data collected over the course of the evening and give them an estimated time as to when you will meet with them to go over the findings.

After the Investigation

It is important to gather as much information related to the location as possible. Our group does extensive historical research on each property we investigate. We choose to do the historical research after the onsite investigation to prevent any team members involved from drawling conclusions based off of prior knowledge.

Our historical research covers information such as previous owners, date the site was originally developed, what the site was used for over the years, and any documented deaths that may have occurred at the location. Your local historical society is a good place to start when conducting research of this nature.

Summary

As with any process or procedure, over time it will need to be revised and improved on. The procedures that we have covered in this chapter are a result of four years of trial and error with out paranormal group. While they may work for us at the moment, you may find that you will need to expand or adapt them to meet your needs and current arsenal of equipment.

9

BRINGING IT ALL TOGETHER

The ultimate goal for any paranormal research team is to capture positive proof of the paranormal. However it is not uncommon for a paranormal team to complete an investigation and spend countless hours reviewing all of the data only to discover the investigation did not produce any type of evidence. It is very easy to become discouraged by this after several investigations resulting in zero evidence. The important thing to remember is that most cases require multiple investigations in order to uncover the truth behind the claims.

Do Not Become Discouraged

If you are like most people interested in the paranormal you probably watch at least one of the many paranormal related TV shows that air each week on your local cable or satellite service provider. One thing that most people don't realize is that these groups perform dozens of investigations but for the most part only the ones with activity make it to the weekly show. The networks involved are looking for ratings and as a result most of the work that goes into setting up and conducting an investigation is either lost or glossed over.

The bottom line to all of this is you must be prepared to investigate a location more than once in order to get to the root of what is really taking place at a location. Even if your team is lucky enough to capture evidence on your first visit it is always a good idea to plan on doing a second investigation if possible to confirm your findings.

Reviewing the Data

The review process is another aspect that is glossed over on most paranormal TV programs. Do not underestimate the amount of time this process takes and plan accordingly. Our team reviews each data set twice to ensure the first person reviewing the data set does not miss anything. By data set, we mean each audio recording, video recording, data logger download, and each investigation log. The more equipment your team owns and uses during the investigation the longer the review process will take. Our team spends roughly 90 to 120 hours reviewing data sets for a typical eight hour investigation. The amount of time for a review is often doubled if we discover multiple pieces of evidence.

Reviewing Audio Evidence

Audio evidence is generally captured one of two ways during an investigation. Most researchers either rely on stand alone digital audio recorders or their video camera's built in microphone. Regardless of the source it is vitally important to maintain the integrity of the original recording at all times.

While the options related to reviewing audio which is part of a video recording are somewhat limited, audio captured on a digital recorder can be analyzed using a number of software packages and techniques. Always make a copy of the digital audio file and use that for your review process. By doing so you will have the freedom to clean suspected EVPs if needed. The two most common software applications used for EVP review are Adobe Audition and Audacity. You can expect to pay around $400 dollars for Adobe's software while Audacity is free open source software. The choice is yours and both applications work well for reviewing audio in search of possible EVPs.

There are numerous techniques that are intended to help clean up an audio recording in an attempt to make the EVP easier to hear and understand. Just remember that when it comes to this type of evidence less is always better. Most researchers consider processed EVP files worthless. We will not go into the techniques used for cleaning audio recordings given the information is readily available on the internet. The information publicly available related to processing an audio file could fill a book all on its own. Just remember to make a copy of the original before reviewing and less is always better with respect to cleaning.

Reviewing Video Evidence

Reviewing video evidence is fairly straight forward. While it is tempting, you should never use fast play back to review video footage captured during an investigation. By doing so you run the risk of missing vital pieces of evidence that may have been captured during the investigation. During the review of this type of evidence you are not only watching the video images for movement of objects, shadows, or anything that seems out of place but you are also listening to the audio associated with it. There are also a number of applications that are available for reviewing video footage but we prefer VLC Media Player for two reasons. First, VLC Media Player has codec's built into the software so it will play just about anything. Second, VLC has a feature that when enabled will automatically detect movement of an object and highlight it for you. While we do not recommend that you rely on this feature for locating evidence, it is a nice feature to use to double check yourself during the review process.

Did You Know? The term *codec* is a blend of the words 'compressor-decompressor' or, more commonly known, 'coder-decoder' and refers to a program capable of encoding and decoding a digital data stream or signal.

Reviewing Photographic Evidence

Photographic evidence is probably the most common form of evidence out there. Digital cameras are inexpensive and readily available, and most groups have a number of them at their disposal. The techniques used for reviewing evidence of this nature are quite extensive and we will not go into the details as there are a number of available sources dedicated to this on the internet already. We will only cover the basics here to give you a starting point and recommend that you take the time to learn as much as you can about the art of photography.

While there are some people who prefer to use film based cameras for paranormal investigation, most use digital cameras because they do not require film development. We will focus our discussion to digital based cameras for this reason. All digital cameras imbed information into each photograph called EXIF metadata. This information can tell you a lot about a photograph such as the camera make, model, image size, resolution, and if the flash was used. There is far more information embedded in the image than you may realize. JPEGsnoop is a software application developed by a gentleman named Calvin Hass that can tell you everything you could ever want to know about the photograph. It can even tell you if the image has been edited or processed. This is a great tool for verifying the validity of paranormal related photos. In fact, the tool is used by forensic scientists on a regular basis. There are many different techniques publicly available on the Internet for cleaning up photographs that contain paranormal anomalies. As with any evidence, the more you process it the less credible it will be.

Correlation of Findings

Correlation is the method of linking evidence in an attempt to validate an observation or theory. We talked about how we use correlation in detail in chapter eight but will quickly review the process again so it is clear. The review process, like the investigation process, is structured in three phases. During the first phase you focus on locating potential paranormal evidence that may have been captured during the investigation.

When you locate a piece of evidence you must log the following information related to that evidence:

- The device the evidence was captured on.
- The location of the device when the evidence was captured.
- The time the evidence was captured.

Once you have reviewed all of the data captured during the investigation you are ready to start phase two of the review process. Phase two involves reviewing the evidence logs in an attempt to identify occurrences. The ultimate goal is to group all evidence that happened around the same time. Over time you will compile a larger data set which you will then review for patterns. If you are able to identify patterns in the occurrences you are ready to form a theory which is what the scientific method is all about. Once you have a theory you will need to test the theory in order to validate it. Phase three is the process of preparing the findings for presentation to the client.

The important thing to remember is never underestimate the amount of time the review process is going to take. Be honest with your clients when giving them an estimate on getting back to them with your findings. Also, take the extra step needed to attempt to correlate your findings as this is the only way to produce verifiable proof of the paranormal.

Presenting Your Findings to the Client

This is probably the most important step in the process of paranormal investigation as far as your client is concerned. Most clients are uncomfortable and on edge due to the phenomena they are dealing with making them eager to have their claims validated. Do not feel obligated or compelled to bring them something in the event your investigation turns up zero evidence. There are many groups out there that fall prey to this scenario and start reaching for anything they feel is paranormal just so they have something to present to the client. Many "orb" photographs that are floating around out there are a result of this. While there is compelling evidence that suggests the possibility

100

that some orb photographs may be related to paranormal events, most of what is presented to clients or the public is explainable. No matter how compelled you feel to produce something for your client always be honest with them.

The reveal process should be well organized and thought out. Provide your clients with as much detail as possible related to the evidence being presented and refrain from jumping to conclusions. It is highly advisable that you leave your clients a copy of the evidence for their review.

In addition to copies of the evidence you should also include the following information:

- Educational material that provides information related to the evidence. For example, if you are leaving the client with an EVP that was captured during their investigation you should also provide information explaining what an EVP is, how they are classified, and information related to the evidences validity.

- Contact information for your group. This information should include the names of the group's founders, a telephone number, and your web address in the event the client needs to contact you at a later date. This requirement can be fulfilled by investing in preprinted presentation binders. Check out the "List of Vendors" on pages 119 - 120 for more information.

- Copy of signed "Media Release Form". In the event your team is able to record and document evidence of the paranormal during an investigation you may want to include the evidence on your website for peer review. In order to do so you will need to get a signed media release form from your client. You should not make the request to have the client sign this form prior to the reveal for two reasons. First, there is no reason to trouble the client for their permission until you are sure you have something to release. Second, the client is dealing with enough stress going in to an investigation. There is no need to add to this stress by having them worry about what you intend on releasing and their privacy.

Try to place yourself in your client's shoes before passing judgment on any aspect of their case. Remember to always use common sense before, during, and after the investigation. Trust and respect needs to be earned. By following these simple rules and the suggested reveal process, you should have no problem gaining either from your clients and your peers.

After the Investigation

We have discussed in great detail how to review the data collected from your investigations, forms that should be signed and collected from your clients, as well as how to present your findings to said clients. Now we will discuss what you should do with the data collected after the investigation. The investigation is not over once you have presented the data to the clients and should not be discarded. The data you collect from your investigations has more value than just posting it to your site for public review. While it may be of interest to the public to be able to review the data captured, the true value in the data collected is derived from the potential it has to substantiate your theories.

BRINGING IT ALL TOGETHER

Summary

Once you are able to accumulate enough data you should start looking for trends that correlate theories to findings. This is the true value of conducting paranormal research using the scientific method. Hard data that backs up your theories is what everyone in the scientific community looks for. Just know that when it comes time to validate your theories by reviewing your accumulated data sets, every aspect of the data will be scrutinized. Make it a point to keep the data in its original pristine state, document every aspect related to how the data was collected, and utilize the same method each time while collecting the data. Consistency is key to strong, irrefutable evidence and will go a long way in supporting your theories and findings.

10

CHOOSING YOUR PATH

The first question that you need to ask yourself is, "What do I hope to gain from my interest in the paranormal?" You need to be honest with yourself when answering this as it's going to be the driving force that determines the path you choose with regards to the methods you use, the team you form or join, and how much time you invest in research. There are many reasons for getting involved in paranormal research and there is no right or wrong reason. However, if you ask anyone who has been in the field for a while, they will tell you there absolutely is "a right way" and "a wrong way" when it comes to conducting investigations.

As a children growing up you probably heard the phrase, "It only takes one bad apple to spoil the bunch". Like most kids, you probably didn't fully understand the full meaning of the phrase. But as an adult the true meaning rings loud and clear. What does this have to do with paranormal research you ask? Well, allow us to explain: one of the upsides to the increased popularity of paranormal research is that people who live in or own places they feel have unexplained activity are now more likely to agree to allow people like us in to investigate. Unfortunately, the down side to this is as the popularity increases so do the number of people out there attempting to do investigations. How can this be a down side you ask? A large number of these people have no experience conducting a professional and organized investigation other than what they have witnessed on TV. They are merely in it for the thrill and have no regard for others in the field when it comes to their actions or how they interact with the property owners. This makes it very hard for groups who take their research seriously to gain access to locations that have potential activity once a group of people as described above has visited the site.

Regardless of how you answered our initial question you need to keep one thing in mind: your actions today will affect all those who follow tomorrow. Honesty is always the best policy, so be up front with potential clients and let them know why you are in the field. Don't make promises or claims to the effect that you are able to rid or "cleanse" a location of anything. Don't mislead them in an attempt to gain access to their property. Make certain that you explain to them there are no real facts regarding the paranormal, only unproven theories. Making false claims not only makes you look bad, but it makes everyone in the field look bad as well.

Another reason why we asked the question, "What do I hope to gain from my interest in the paranormal?" is that it will help determine how you should approach joining or establishing a group. If your answer is along the lines of "it's fun and I enjoy doing it when I have time" then you may want to consider looking for a local group and trying to establish a connection with them. You will find it far less expensive and time consuming than trying to establish your own team. If you are still set on starting your own group then you need to be well prepared for the amount of time and the expense that is associated with doing so. Conversely, if your answer was along the lines of "I want to have control over the methods used during the investigations I'm involved with" then you are treating this as more than a hobby and will most likely be interested in forming your own team. This was the driving force that compelled us to found our team, *The Supernatural Research Group*. The only thing that we want to point out to those of you who fall into this category is it is highly frowned upon by those in the paranormal community to charge for any investigative services. You need to be prepared to work long and hard to establish your group in a positive manner within your community. Yes, there are those who do earn a living from their work in this field, but they are part of a small elite group of who have been working in the field for many years.

Unforeseen Obstacles

One thing you won't learn from watching any of the programs on TV is the actual expense involved or the time required to do an adequate job. Granted there are sites and publications out there that state "The only tools a paranormal investigator really needs is a notebook, flashlight and a friend to conduct an investigation", and this may be true for those who are merely involved in paranormal research as a hobby or for the thrill. For those of you who are serious about conducting scientific based paranormal research, you will need far greater resources at your disposal than you may realize.

CHOOSING YOUR PATH

In our first year, *The Supernatural Research Group* spent well over $3,500.00 on equipment alone. That figure doesn't include the costs associated with developing, hosting and maintaining our website, purchasing our business cards, t-shirts and hats for our team members, as well as brochures, letter head, and the envelopes we used to solicit potential clients for the opportunity to investigate their home or business. Why did we spend so much money so early into our existence you ask? Well the simple truth is competition. There are seven paranormal groups located in the same county where we reside who are actively conducting paranormal research. There are probably more, but the seven that we mentioned are active and have a web presence established. We also needed to expand our inventory of tools used during our investigations. In the event you haven't noticed, you will be hard pressed to find any team with a paranormal website that doesn't have a page dedicated to the equipment they use during their investigations. It seems more like a competition than anything, but we will be the first to admit that the amount and type of equipment doesn't automatically make an individual a better investigator. However, let's take a moment and look at this from the perspective of a potential client who is doing a little research into who they can call to come into their home or business to help explain some of the strange things that have been witnessed over the years. We are willing to bet the last place this person is going to turn to locate someone who can help them is their local phone directory, although we are sure somewhere out there you can probably find a paranormal group listed in the yellow pages. Up until the popularity explosion that resulted from the countless paranormal TV shows, these folks more than likely turned to their family and friends for help. So based on the fact that most prospective clients are going to base what they know off what they may have seen on TV, potential clients are more likely to use the internet or word of mouth to locate a paranormal research team. Having said that, should they in fact turn to the internet to find a group, they are more than likely going to look for things they have seen on TV. This is why so many groups have gone to the trouble of listing their arsenal of equipment. It is nothing more than a means of validating their existence in the field. Unfortunately, unless you have your own TV series, this is a fact of life each paranormal team has to come to terms with if they intend to compete for locations to investigate.

Up to this point we have only talked about the monetary commitment that is required to get your team established. However, this isn't the only thing a prospective paranormal investigator needs to overcome if they want to be successful. The amount of time, in our opinion, is the most underestimated thing new investigators fail to take into consideration. Unless you are independently wealthy and have more time than you know what to do with, you are going to be working full time and conducting your research as time permits. Paranormal research will be part time at best provided you don't have a family to look after. Our point here is don't underestimate the amount of time it is going to take to establish your group in your community. If you hope to do more than two or three investigation per year, you will need to work hard to make it happen.

CHOOSING YOUR PATH

Forming a Paranormal Group

This topic seems pretty straight forward doesn't it? Well there is more to it than meets the eye and you should not take the process too lightly. In addition to the time and monetary factors we have already discussed, forming a paranormal research group requires mastering the skills and becoming very familiar with the equipment you have chosen, all of which we discussed in previous chapters of this book. You will need to recruit honest and trustworthy people for your team and train these individuals to ensure your methods and procedures are followed. Your friends and family are one possible source for recruitment of potential team members, but you should keep in mind that the people you choose for your team must be willing to take direction and follow the methods that you have established for your group. Your website will be another source to draw from so you should have a page or section dedicated to recruiting. A great location for this is on the same page where you provide the background information for each of your current members. By doing so, prospective applicants will be able to get a good idea of what your team stands for and who they may be working with in the field if selected. The final decision regarding who will be admitted into your group lies solely with you, the team founder. You should however, make it a point to include your existing team members in the selection process because they will need to work along side anyone chosen as a new member. The selection process should include an application which is filled out by all prospective members, an interview process, followed by an initial probationary period of 60 to 90 days in which all new team members have an opportunity to show that they get along with the rest of the team, follow direction, and have the ability to learn and adapt to the methods of your group.

Your group will need a name which implies more than you realize and should be well thought out, as it will be responsible for helping to establish a first impression with potential clients. We can't tell you how many times we have come across a group who attempts to add to the fear factor by using a name that would make for a better movie title than a paranormal research group. The bottom line is you should choose a name for your group that is going to convey a clear meaning and shows professionalism. Our group's name was chosen because it states everything we are about; The Supernatural Research Group. We are a group of like-minded people who enjoy researching supernatural claims. We purposely stayed away from the term paranormal, as we felt it suggested that our research was limited to only ghosts. While 70% of our investigations are focused on paranormal research, we have members who spend much of their time researching legends and folklore as well.

Building a Paranormal Team Website

Once you found a few people for your team and have chosen a name for the group, you will need to focus on establishing a positive presence in your community. One of the best ways to do this is with a web site that will give potential clients all of the information about your group they could ever want. At the very minimum you will want to include a separate page dedicated to telling site visitors about the following:

- Group's Mission Statement.

- Biographical information on each of your team members.
- Information related to how your team conducts its investigations.
- The geographic area your team covers.
- General information related to the methods and the type of equipment your team uses during investigations.

It is also a good idea to provide potential clients with as much educational information related to the paranormal as possible. This allows them to conduct their own research before making the decision to get an outside group of individuals involved. And it shows that your team is dedicated to the field.

Promoting Your Paranormal Website

If you have spent any time looking into generating traffic for your site it won't take long to realize that the process can be overwhelming to say the least. Another thing that quickly jumps out is the fact that it wouldn't take much time to sink a pile of money into the process as well. Most SEO (Search Engine Optimization) programs are geared toward sites that are selling a product or service. While your team does offer a service, that service doesn't seem to fit within most SEO resellers categories. We have invested close to $200.00 with such services only to realize zero return for our investment. Below is a recent report from a service that has failed to produce results for two sites that we have registered with them:

Web Traffic Report
for the week of 4/11 – 4/17
Site Name The Supernatural Research Group
Site URL http://www.tsrg.org
Total hits 0
From last Mail 0
Credits 1000
State   Enabled
Date   Received
04.11.2010 0
04.12.2010 0
04.13.2010 0
04.14.2010 0
04.15.2010 0
04.16.2010 0
04.17.2010 0
Paranormal Related Content

Figure 1.8 Web Traffic Results

At first glance you might think, well… it's only one week. But the fact is we have had similar results to the above report for four weeks straight. While there may be SEO sites out there that do a better job, we strongly feel that if you put the following techniques to work you will see a far greater return on your investment. Speaking of investment, the only thing these techniques are going to cost you is a little time.

Generating Traffic

While the ultimate goal of any paranormal group's website is to generate leads for locations to investigate, we shouldn't lose focus on the other roles our sites play as well. One of the most beneficial things about each team's paranormal web site is it gives paranormal researchers an opportunity to collaborate on their investigations and findings. Every paranormal web site should have a section dedicated to investigations. This section should be easy to locate from anywhere on the site and should contain, at the very least, a list of past and future investigations your team is involved with. This shows anyone who visits your site that your group is active, trusted and willing to contribute to the field.

Now, let's get right to the heart of this matter, which is driving traffic to your site. There are numerous ways to increase web traffic to your site. The following gives you a general overview of some of the methods that are available to promote your site that will only require your time and little to no money.

Search Engine Submission:

Your first step should be to register your web site with each of the major search engines. The major players are: Google, yahoo, Bing, Ask, and "The Open Directory" project. Unfortunately, most of these search engines have limitations on how you can register your site. Google should be your first stop and they offer a great selection of tools to help you monitor where the traffic that hits your site originates from. Best of all, Google's tools are 100% free and can be found by going to the following URL:

http://www.google.com/analytics/

Before you jump into the registration process for your website, you need two very important pieces of code to make this process successful. All search engines are set up to use a specific file to help navigate your site. This file is called a sitemap and is in XML format. It not only tells the search engines how to crawl the site, but it also provides a summary of the content of your site as well. Now don't panic! You do not need to know anything about XML or creating the file as there are free tools available that will do all of the work for you. You will however

113

need to have your content in place and your site ready for visitors before you begin the submission process. Once you are ready to open your site up to the world, visit the following site and complete the form with the information that is requested.

http://www.xml-sitemaps.com/

Now that you have the "sitemap.xml" file saved to your local computer you will need to upload the file to the root of your web server, which is generally the "www" directory and is displayed when you connect to your site with your favorite FTP client. If you don't have a FTP client installed, you can download a free one called "FileZilla" from http://filezilla-project.org. This free FTP client is feature rich and will make your life much easier when it comes to updating your website.

The second equally important piece of code that you will need is a file called "robots.txt". This file is nothing more than a simple text file that contains commands that dictate what files and directories a search engine's robot or crawler is allowed to index. Think of it as a list of rules for a search engine that details what the search engine agent is and is not allowed to do on your site. This file is intended to prevent private directories and files from showing up in search results to the general public. This comes in very handy for those of you who want to carve out a special area on your website for members only. Below is an example of what this file should contain at a minimum:

```
User-Agent: *
Disallow: /<DIRECTORY_NAME>/
Disallow: /<FILE_NAME>
Allow: /
sitemap: http://www.<YOUR_DOMAIN>/sitemap.xml
```

Figure 1.9 Sample Robots.txt file

CHOOSING YOUR PATH

You will need to replace "<DIRECTORY_NAME>" or "<FILE_NAME>" with a directory or file that you want to keep private. Also replace "<YOUR_DOMAIN>" with your actual domain name. You should replace everything between the double quote marks. After you have created and uploaded your "sitemap.xml" and "robots.txt" files, it's time to start registering your website with the major search engines. The following list of URL's is intended to help you with registering your website with the major search engines we discussed earlier:

Google:
http://www.google.com/addurl/

Yahoo:
http://search.yahoo.com/info/submit.html

Bing:
http://www.bing.com/webmaster/WebmasterAddSitesPage.aspx

The Open Directory Project:
http://www.dmoz.org/add.html

Ask:
Ask.com does not permit direct submission of your site. You will get listed if you use a "sitemap.xml" file and have reciprocal links.

Reciprocal Links

Reciprocal links are web links to other websites that you agree to display on your site in exchange for the webmaster of that site displaying a web link to your site. Reciprocal links will do two things for you if done right, they will help improve your ranking with most major search engines, and they provide opportunities to gain traffic to your website from visitors of the referring site. In order for this to be effective you need to make sure that you only exchange links with sites that share the same subject matter as your site. Do not place web links on your site to websites that sell shoes, car insurance, or anything unrelated to your site's content. Not only will this be a waste of time for you but it will work against you with respect to your positioning with the search engines. Most paranormal groups will be more than happy to add a link to your site in exchange for you doing the same in return provided your site is clean and professional. Many webmasters will shy away from web sites that are hosted on free hosting services since those services require each domain to display their ads. If you do not have the budget to pay for web hosting you should consider hosting your site with X10hosting, http://x10hosting.com/freehosting.php, which offers an impressive ad free service.

Paranormal Social Networks

Another great way to drive traffic to your site for free is registering and participating with one or more of the many paranormal social websites on the World Wide Web. Doing a Google search on "Paranormal Social" will return dozens of sites that offer free membership. Take some time and create an account on several of them making sure you list the URL for your group's website in your profile. These sites offer a medium for like minded people to discuss anything and everything related to the paranormal field. You can increase your odds of gaining traffic by contributing to some of the topics being discussed and who knows, you might even learn something you didn't know.

CHOOSING YOUR PATH

Here is a list of some of the Paranormal Social Sites for you to start out with (there are many more sites out there for the choosing):

MyPara Paranormal Social Network:
Paranormal social network that connects people who are interested in hauntings and ghosts. Upload videos, blogs, and have a custom profile.

http://www.mypara.net/

Supernatural Connections:
Supernatural Connections is a free social network community for those interested in the supernatural, the paranormal or any type of unusual phenomena.

http://www.supernaturalconnections.com/

Paralore.com:
Online community dedicated the all things paranormal.

http://www.paralore.com/

Social Media Advertising

Don't overlook the awesome potential for generating leads from social media networks such as Facebook, MySpace, and Twitter. Take some time and create accounts on each of these sites for your group. Make sure you include background information about your group, the URL for your team's site, as well as the contact info for your group on each site.

Local Advertising

Another option that is available to any group is local advertising. While the cost of placing your groups name and info on a billboard may place it out of reach, placing a classified ad in your local newspaper might be an option for your group. Many newspapers offer special rates for non-profit groups located in their service territory. If you are willing to invest $100.00 or so you're advertising options may surprise you. Even if you are not in a position to invest in advertising for your group at the moment, you should keep this option in the back of your mind for a later date.

Summary

We have covered many topics in this chapter including more than a few options that are available to you and your group to drive visitors to your site. All of the aforementioned information and techniques will help you build a solid paranormal team as well as increase web traffic to your site. Increased traffic will help to improve the sites ranking with the major search engines. This in turn brings valuable traffic to your site which may lead to possible locations for your group to investigate. Just keep in mind that while this will not happen overnight, it will happen. All it takes is a little time well spent getting your name out there so people can find you.

SAMPLE FORMS

The following forms are being provided as a point of reference for you while creating your own version. These forms are considered good practice as they help protect you and your group as well as the property owner from the possibility of future litigation that may arise.

By no means should these forms be considered legally binding without first consulting an attorney in your state as laws may differ by location. These forms are intended to give you a general idea of some of the things you should consider prior to undertaking any type of paranormal investigation.

Disclaimer:

If you choose to use the included sample forms as is, you do so at your own risk. The materials in this book are provided "as is" without warranty of any kind, either expressed or implied, including, but not limited to, the implied warranties of merchantability, fitness for a particular purpose, or non-infringement. Some jurisdictions do not allow the exclusion of implied warranties, so the above exclusion may not apply to you.

In no event shall the Authors of this book be liable for any damages whatsoever, including special, indirect, consequential or incidental damages or damages for loss of profits, revenue, use, or data whether brought in contract or tort, arising out of or connected with any information or the use, reliance upon or performance of any material contained in this publication.

Membership Application

<GROUP LOGO HERE>

<GROUP NAME HERE>

Team Member Application Form

Thank you for your interest in becoming a <GROUP NAME> team member. We take great pride in our research and the good name that we have worked very hard to build in this field. Reputation is the only thing a team such as ours has at the end of the day. Having said that, We want to take this opportunity to elaborate a bit on why we are asking for the information that is included in this application.

<GROUP NAME> has gone to great lengths to gain the trust of our current and future clients. As such, we feel it is our responsibility to ensure that each and every member of our organization meets certain criteria before being allowed to represent the group as a whole to the general public.

PRIVACY ACT STATEMENT AND CONSENT

Principal Purpose and Routine Uses
The information collected on this form will be used for the sole purpose of conducting security risk assessments on <GROUP NAME> Members and applicants. As part of this assessment, the collected data may also be used to assist in determining approval, denial, revocation or renewal of access to the <GROUP NAME> resources and the authorization to receive or review <GROUP NAME> sensitive information. Information provided by you will be protected and used in strict compliance with the US Privacy Act and will be destroyed or returned upon separation from <GROUP NAME>.

Effects of Nondisclosure or Falsification
Completion of this application is voluntary. However, failure to provide the requested information may result in your application being rejected for membership in <GROUP NAME>. Knowingly falsifying or concealing information requested on this form will result in your application being rejected or your membership revoked. <GROUP NAME> will conduct a general criminal background investigation on each applicant to ensure the safety of its members and clients.

Consent
By signing the <GROUP NAME> Membership Application Form, I hereby authorize <GROUP NAME> to obtain and verify any information relevant to assessing my suitability for team membership. This information may include, but is not limited to, law enforcement and intelligence information. I further authorize <GROUP NAME> to disclose information obtained in connection with my security risk assessment in order to verify the accuracy or completeness of the information I have provided. Other than to verify my information, I do not authorize <GROUP NAME> to disclose for the purpose of conducting my security risk assessment, information provided by me on this form absent my further written consent.

_____ Date: _____
PRINTED NAME

_____ Date: _____
SIGNATURE

Page one of four

SAMPLE FORMS

Membership Application - Continued

<GROUP NAME> Membership Application

Name (Applicant): _____

Employer: _____

Title: _____

Business Address: _____

City: _____ State: _____

Zip Code: _____

Home Address: _____

City: _____ State: _____

Zip Code: _____

Email Address: _____

Home Phone: _____

Cell Phone: _____

Date of Birth: _____ Place of birth: _____

Drivers License #: _____ State of Issue: _____

Gender: **Male / Female** (Please circle one)

Have you ever been arrested for, charged with, or convicted of a felony or non-traffic misdemeanor? If yes, please attach an explanation of the occurrence(s) making sure to include dates, agencies involved, case numbers, disposition, and any additional information that you feel would assist us in making a membership decision (Check one):

☐ Yes (Number of pages Attached) _____ ☐ No

Have you ever been a member of another paranormal group? If yes, please list group(s)

_____

Are you currently with a paranormal group? If yes, please list group(s)

_____

How many years have you been conducting paranormal investigations? (If none please enter zero)

_____

Please list any equipment that you currently own which is used for paranormal investigation:

_____
_____

Please tell us why you feel you would be a good paranormal investigator:

_____
_____
_____
_____
_____

Do you have any of the following abilities: Precognition, Psychic, Psychokinesis, Telekinesis or other? If yes, please explain:

_____
_____
_____

2 of 4

Page two of four

Membership Application - Continued

<GROUP NAME> Membership Application

What are your religious beliefs?

_____

_____

What experience do you have in the paranormal field?

_____

_____

Why are you seeking membership with <GROUP NAME> as a paranormal researcher?

_____

_____

What expectations do you have regarding your membership with <GROUP NAME>?

_____

_____

What areas of the paranormal most intrigue you?

_____

_____

What role do you see yourself in if you are selected as a full member of <GROUP NAME>?

_____

_____

Please read the following disclosure and indicate your acceptance of the following below:
Applicant understands that their involvement with "<GROUP NAME>" is strictly voluntary. They should also understand that they will not receive any type of monetary compensation for their time or involvement with the group.

Applicant understands and agrees that <GROUP NAME> is not to be commercially exploited as a forum to market products or services and that doing so may result in the revocation of Applicants membership in <GROUP NAME>. Applicant, if accepted as a <GROUP NAME> member, agrees to act in a manner consistent with the <GROUP NAME> By-Laws, as the By-Laws may be amended from time to time, as well as any other duly enacted requirements of <GROUP NAME>.
Applicant requirements:
- US Citizen by birth as defined by 8 USC §1401-§1409, OR US Citizen by Naturalization as defined by 8 USC §1421-§1459;
- Over 18 years of age on the date of completion of this Application;
- Consent to a records check that yields a satisfactory result as determined by <GROUP NAME> in its sole discretion, OR posses a Qualifying Substitute;
- Consent to periodic re-confirmation of membership requirements;
- Agree to and complete this <GROUP NAME> Membership Application Form;

Applicant acknowledges that their affiliation with <GROUP NAME> may be disclosed by <GROUP NAME> to another <GROUP NAME> member or the general public. Applicant may choose to protect from public disclosure their affiliation with <GROUP NAME>, and request that <GROUP NAME> and <GROUP NAME> Partners also protect from public disclosure the Applicant's affiliation with <GROUP NAME>.

May <GROUP NAME> publicly disclose Applicants association with <GROUP NAME>? (Check one):
☐ Yes   ☐ No

3 of 4

Page three of four

SAMPLE FORMS

Membership Application - Continued

<GROUP NAME> Membership Application

Consent

By signing this <GROUP NAME> Membership Application Form, I hereby authorize <GROUP NAME> to obtain and verify any information relevant to assessing my suitability as a team member or to access, possess, use, receive or transfer sensitive <GROUP NAME> Information. This information may include, but is not limited to, case and client information and sensitive <GROUP NAME> policies and procedures. I further authorize <GROUP NAME> to disclose information obtained in connection with my security risk assessment in order to verify the accuracy or completeness of the information I have provided to <GROUP NAME>. Other than to verify my information, I do not authorize <GROUP NAME> to disclose for the purpose of conducting my security risk assessment information provided by me on this form absent my further written consent.

_____ Date: _____
PRINTED NAME

_____ Date: _____
SIGNATURE

Note: Please include a copy of a State or Government issued photo ID with your application.

4 of 4

Page four of four

Ghost Hunting From A to Z – A Scientific Approach

Permission to Investigate Form

<INSERT GROUP LOGO>   **<GROUP NAME HERE>**

LAND/DWELLING OWNER PERMISSION FOR USE OF PREMISES OR LAND

Permission Request From:

_____
CASE MANAGER NAME
Group Name
Address
City, State Zip Code
Telephone Number

The following <Group Name> owned vehicles may be onsite during the investigation:

Vehicle Make:_____, Year: _____, Color: _____ License Plate No.: _____

Vehicle Make:_____, Year: _____, Color: _____ License Plate No.: _____

Vehicle Make:_____, Year: _____, Color: _____ License Plate No.: _____

Vehicle Make:_____, Year: _____, Color: _____ License Plate No.: _____

Number of investigators onsite: _____

Purpose of visit: To conduct scientific research related to the paranormal, to include but not limited to, recording and documenting video, audio, images, temperature and energy level readings as they relate to paranormal investigation.

Number of days requesting permission to investigate: _____

Proposed Date(s) for investigation: From ___ / ___ / ___ To ___ / ___ / ___

I agree to conduct myself safely, responsibly and lawfully, respecting the landowner, property and others using it. I accept the responsibilities which are part of these activities which I pursue. I agree to comply with the instructions of the landowner while on this property. In consideration for said permission I am including a signed WAIVER AND RELEASE FROM LIABILITY form. If you require changes to the enclosed form please make the changes on the enclosed form and return it for correction. A completed; correct copy will be provided prior to our arrival if granting permission.

I understand the risks and liabilities associated with conducting paranormal investigations and take full responsibility for myself and my team members during our investigation.

_____ Date: _____
PRINTED NAME

_____
SIGNATURE

Please complete and return this page in the postage paid envelope provided if granting permission to investigate

1 of 2

Page one of two

124

SAMPLE FORMS

Permission to Investigate Form - Continued

PERMISSION TO OCCUPY PREMISSES

I hereby grant permission to <Group Founder's Name>, Founder of <Group Name>, and members of his/her party to enter and occupy my property for the purpose listed below. He/She has agreed to act safely, responsibly and lawfully and to accept responsibility for his/her groups actions.

Dates:

From ___ / ___ / ___   To ___ / ___ / ___

Limitations:

_____

_____

_____

_____

_____

_____

_____

_____

_____

Land / Dwelling Owners Name: _____

    Address: _____

        _____

        _____

    Telephone Number: _____

_____ Date: _____
PRINTED NAME

_____
SIGNATURE

VISITOR COPY ~ NOT TRANSFERABLE

2 of 2

Page two of two

Ghost Hunting From A to Z – A Scientific Approach

Waiver and Release from Liability Form

<GROUP NAME>

WAIVER AND RELEASE FROM LIABILITY FOR OWNER OF PREMISES OR LAND

I, _____, HEREBY WAIVE AND RELEASE, indemnify, hold harmless
<GROUP FOUNDER NAME> Member Name
and forever discharge _____ from any and all claims, demands,
Land / Building Owner Name
debts, contracts, expenses, causes of action, lawsuits, damages and liabilities, of every kind and nature,
whether known or unknown, in law or equity, that I ever had or may have, arising from or in any way related to
paranormal investigation activities on the premises of land owned by
_____(Property Owner/Manager) in the County of
Land / Building Owner Name
_____, in the State of _____ provided that this waiver of
County   State
liability does not apply to any acts of gross negligence, or intentional, willful or wanton misconduct.
I understand that the activities that I will participate in are inherently dangerous and may cause serious or
grievous injuries, including bodily injury, damage to personal property and/or death. On behalf of myself, my
heirs, assigns and next of kin, I waive all claims for damages, injuries and death sustained to me or my
property that I may have against the aforementioned released party to such activity.

By this Waiver, I assume any risk, and take full responsibility and waive any claims of personal injury, death or
damage to personal property owned by _____,
Land / Building Owner Name
including but not limited to the act of paranormal investigation on the land or in any dwelling, using the land in
any manner, form or fashion, and engaging in any outdoor activities or other related activities on and off the
premises.

This WAIVER AND RELEASE contains the entire agreement between the parties, and supersedes any prior
written or oral agreements between them concerning the subject matter of this WAIVER AND RELEASE. The
provisions of this WAIVER AND RELEASE may be waived, altered, amended or repealed, in whole or in part, only
upon the prior written consent of all parties.

I have read, understand and fully agree to the terms of this WAIVER AND RELEASE. I understand and confirm
that by signing this WAIVER AND RELEASE I have given up considerable future legal rights. I have signed this
Agreement freely, voluntarily, under no duress or threat of duress, without inducement, promise or guarantee
being communicated to me. My signature is proof of my intention to execute a complete and unconditional
WAIVER AND RELEASE of all liability to the full extent of the law. I am 18 years of age or older and mentally
competent to enter into this waiver. This agreement and its terms and provisions will include any minors who
accompany me or who are under my care. I further agree that I shall assume responsibility for watching and
caring for minor's safety and guarding against all hazards, natural or manmade, whether expressly mentioned in
this WAIVER AND RELEASE or otherwise.

_____ Date: _____
PRINTED NAME

_____ Date: _____
SIGNATURE

1

Page one of one

SAMPLE FORMS

Media Release Authorization Form

<GROUP LOGO>   **<GROUP NAME>**

Media Release Authorization

The members of **<GROUP_NAME>** respect your right to privacy. All of your personal information **WILL** be kept confidential. **<GROUP_NAME>** would like to use some or all of the information and evidence collected during the investigation for possible inclusion on our website, in newsletters and other future media considerations. Please check the level of confidentiality you are comfortable with or provide detailed release instructions in the space provided:

☐	**<GROUP_NAME>** may not release any part of the investigation to the public. This includes but is not limited to photos, audio or video recordings.
☐	**<GROUP_NAME>** may use and release any information or evidence recorded during the investigation provided that the identity of witnesses, clients and the exact address of the location is excluded.
☐	**<GROUP_NAME>** is free to use and release any/all information and evidence collected during their investigation of my property.
☐	Other – Please specify your requirements here:

I hereby agree to release, defend, and hold harmless **<GROUP_NAME>** and subordinates, including any firm publishing and/or distributing the finished product in whole or in part, whether on paper or via electronic media, from and against any claims, damages or liability arising from or related to the use of the photographs, video, audio or historical back ground information either intentionally or otherwise, that may occur or be produced from results obtained during their investigation of my property.

Date: _____

Name (Please Print): _____

Address: _____
(Street)   (City)   (State/Province)   (Zip Code)

Signature: _____ Date: _____

Witness: _____ Date: _____

1

Page one of one

127

LIST OF VENDORS

Creepy Hollow Gear – Site owned and operated by Paul Bradford, investigator on "Ghost Hunters International" that sells various tools used during paranormal investigations.

Telephone Number: Not Available
Web Address: http://www.creepyhollowgear.com

Fourier Home – Manufacturers of the "MultiLogPro" and other Data loggers.

Telephone Number: 877-266-4066
Web Address: http://www.fourier-sys.com

Ghost-Mart – Distributor of items and equipment related to paranormal research located out of Huntington, WV.

Telephone Number: 304-513-4216
Web Address: www.ghost-mart.com

NVRUSA – Distributor of CCTV Camera's and DVR's.

Telephone Number: 800-473-4418
Web Address: http://www.nvrusa.com

JoeUSA.com – Affordable web hosting and domain registration services.

Telephone Number: 321-610-7797
Web Address: http://www.joeusa.com

LIST OF USEFUL VENDORS

Professional Measurement – Your one stop shop for test and measurement products. Inventor and distributor of the Mel Meter line of EMF meters.

Telephone Number: 888-344-0111
Web Address: http://www.pro-measure.com

Queensboro – Excellent source for embroidered or screen printed hats, shirts and jackets.

Telephone Number: 800-847-4478
Web Address: http://www.queensboro.com

$AVE | Use the following URL exactly as illustrated below and get $25.00 off your first order from Queensboro if you are a new customer.

http://www.queensboro.com/ref/OROCQQOSMMC

SpecterCam – Manufactuere of Full Spectrum CCTV cameras and accessories. The site is packed with good information related to recording video. Tell Keith that TSRG sent you!

Web Address: http://www.spectercam.com

The Ghost Hunter Store – Ghost hunting gear for sale by people who use the equipment.

Telephone Number: 609-261-2361
Web Address: http://theghosthunterstore.com

Vistaprint – Excellent source for business cards, letter head and other printed materials at a very reasonable price.

Telephone Number: Not Available
Web Address: http://www.vistaprint.com

X10hosting – Excellent source for free website hosting.

Telephone Number: 888-910-9668
Web Address: http://x10hosting.com/freehosting.php

Glossary of Supernatural Terms

Abacomancy: A method of divination using patterns of dust. In some cases the dust is from the remains of the recently deceased.

Abaddon: The name of the demon in Revelations 9.11 known as the angel of the bottomless pit.

Abductee: Someone who claims to have been abducted. In paranormal terms this typically refers to abduction by extraterrestrials.

Abigor: The name of a demon who has the power to see into the future and provide military aid.

Abominable Snowman:, Is a tall ape-like creature said to inhabit the Himalayan Mountains. The North American version is the Bigfoot.

Abracadabra: A word which is used as a popular magical incantation. Originated as a Kabalistic charm.

Abrasax: A mystical word linked to the solar cycle. It expresses the number 365 geometrically.

Active Haunt: A type of haunting which refers to activity in which a spirit or entity interacts with the living. Characteristics of this type of activity range from direct responses to questions asked during an EVP session, to being touched, pushed or even scratched when provoked.

Adamastor: The name of a spirit inhabiting the Cape of Good Hope who prophesizes doom for those sailing beyond the cape towards India.

Adept: A person skilled in the ways of the occult.

Adytum: A Greek word describing the holiest part of a temple. In occultism it describes the holiest area of an initiation center.

Aeromancy: The art of predicting the future by observing atmospheric conditions such as wind and cloud formations. It is also know as austromancy.

Aetites: A stone said to be found in the throat or stomach of an eagle. It is supposed to have magical properties which can provide protection during childbirth, prevent miscarriages and prevent premature births.

Agathodemon: A benevolent spirit with a serpent's body and human head, worshipped by ancient Egyptians.

Alastor: An avenging deity or spirit. Greek in origin. A male version of the Greek mythological deity Nemesis.

Alberich: In Scandinavian mythology, the King of the Dwarves and the guardian of the treasures of the Nibelungs.

Alchemy: A form of pseudo-science aimed at converting base metals and other materials into gold.

Alectromancy: The art of divination by using a bird or several birds. Traditionally this involves using a rooster. Various aspects of the bird(s) behavior are used in the divination process.

Aleuromancy: The art of divination using flour. In one technique, sentences are written on pieces of paper, rolled up in flour and distributed amongst participants to tell them their future. Another method involves reading the residue left in a flour/water container. Fortune cookies are an example of Aleuromancy.

Alien: An extraterrestrial being, i.e. from some location other than the earth.

Alien Abduction: A phenomena in which people claim to have been abducted by aliens, usually an unpleasant experience, often involving painful procedures. See also **Abductee.**

Alma: The term is Mongolian and it means 'wild man'. It describes a Big Foot like hominid that supposedly inhabits the Caucasus and Pamir Mountains of central Asia. There are also claims that it exists in the Altai Mountains of southern Mongolia.

Alomancy: The art of divination using salt in a similar way to aleuromancy.

Alphitomancy: An ancient Greek method of judging a person's innocence or guilt by feeding them a specially-prepared barley loaf. If the accused suffers from stomach irritation or pain, they are deemed guilty.

Amulet: An object used to ward off evil. Amulets can take many forms such as a crucifix, crystal, or St. Michael medal. Regardless of the form they take they are always designed to protect a person from harm.

Ancient Astronauts: Extraterrestrial beings that are said to have visited Earth in the distant past helping early humans develop culture and technology.

Angel: An immortal being who acts as an intermediary or messenger between God and mortals. Although popular culture usually portrays angels as good, they can be good or evil.

Animal PSI: The apparent ability of animals to exhibit psychic powers such as clairvoyance, telepathy and even psychokinesis. Reported examples include the ability to sense impending danger, sensing the proximity of an owner, sensing harm to an owner at a distance, and to navigate unknown territory.

Anthropomancy: A method of divination by human sacrificial entrails. This practice was sometimes known as splanchomancy.

Antichrist: The demon who is predicted to precede the Second Coming of Christ in the book of Revelations. He is considered to be the adversary of Christ. Appearing much like Christ in his ways but being deceptive and evil in nature.

Apparition: The visible and sometimes physically tangible manifestation of a spiritual or psychic energy.

Apport: The occurrence of an object, inanimate or living, that appears to be transported from one closed of area to another without any apparent cause.

Arcanum: Something hidden, or secret information known only to a certain group. The plural, arcane, refers to the varied knowledge of occult lore.

Archangel: The term archangel refers to the highest ranking of the angels. From a religious perspective the concept of archangel's are found in Judaism, Christianity, Islam, Wicca and Zoroastrianism.

Area 51: Popular name given to part of a secret military base in North America. It is located in the southern portion of Nevada near Groom Lake. It has been long rumored to be involved with extraterrestrial beings and/or technology.

Ariolater: One who practices divination. Also called seers, soothsayers and diviners.

Arithmomancy: Similar to numerology, the practice of divination using numbers. Using numbers to predict the outcome of situations was popular in ancient Greece.

Ark of the Covenant: A gold chest said to contain the stone tablets upon which the Ten Commandments were inscribed by God.

Aset Ka: A spiritual society and metaphysical order of mysteries, which is believed to be founded by an entity known as Aset. This order is also believed to be one of the most influential Kemetic orders as well as vampiric movements inside the occult underground of Europe.

Astragalomancy: A method of divination by throwing dice or bones marked with letters and numbers.

Astral: A vague term that is used to describe the fabric of the heavens or another realm.

Astral Body: The spiritual version of the physical body.

Astral Plane: The dimension inhabited by higher spiritual beings, invisible to humans but visited during sleep, trance states and after death.

Astral Projection: A term used to describe any type of out-of-body experience.

Astrology: The study of celestial bodies and their influence on one's personality, affairs and other related matters.

Atlantis: A legendary island, according to Plato, which was said to have existed around 9000 BC and inhabited by an advanced civilization. There are mixed opinions on whether or not Atlantis existed at all. There are various theories as to its demise that includes everything from volcanoes to the inhabitants themselves accidentally destroying the island with their own technology.

Augur: A diviner who foretold the future by observing animal behaviors.

Aura: An apparent envelope of energy that surrounds human individuals. Under normal circumstances it's invisible but claimed to be seen by psychics and aura photographers.

Austromancy: A diviner or soothsayer who predicts events based on observing the wind and cloud formations.

Automatic Writing: The practice of writing text while in a trance or state of altered consciousness. Used by mediums to communicate with the spirit world.

Axinomancy: A method of divination involving an axe; for example, heating the axe in the embers of a fire to interpret the color and shapes. Another form involves throwing the ax into the ground or swinging into a table or tree and interpreting the angle of the handle.

Backward Blessing: The practice of reciting the Lord's Prayer backwards, said to invoke the Devil. It is also used to describe the act of placing a curse on someone.

Balneum Mariae: A type of double-cooker originally used in alchemy. It is also known as a bain-marie, which is a French term used to describe a piece of equipment used to heat objects slowly to a fixed temperature. It was believed that this best simulated the conditions existing deep underground where precious metals were formed.

Banshee: The Banshee originates in Irish culture. The name comes from the Irish word bean 'si' for 'woman of the fairy mounds'. It is a spirit in the classification of fairies in Irish mythology of female gender. It is primarily seen as a warning that death is near. The concept of a banshee is most often associated with the banshee's 'scream'. According to Irish myth, the banshee cries or wails around a house or family if someone is about to die. In certain cases the cry of the banshee, for a family member that died away from home, was the first warning to a family that their loved one had passed away. According to tradition the banshee could only cry or sing for the death of five major Irish families. They are the O'Briens, the O'Connors, the O'Gradys, the O'Neills and the Kavanaghs. Banshees are also common in Scottish folklore.

Basilisk: The mythical king of serpents and is said to kill with a glance.

Beelzebub: Translates literally as "Lord of the Flies", regarded as one of the seven princes of hell. Referred to in Matthew 12:24 as the "Prince of the Devils".

Belomancy: A method of divination using arrows. Messages are either attached to arrows or inscribed on the arrow. One method requires the arrows to be shot and the one that travels the farthest is taken to be the truth. The other method involves placing the arrows in a quiver, which is worn on the back, and then drawing the arrow which contains the answer to the question.

Belphegor: A demon that helps people make ingenious discoveries that will make them rich thereby pushing the human towards the sin of Sloth.

Bermuda Triangle: An area in the Atlantic Ocean defined by Bermuda, Florida and Puerto Rico. Various paranormal events have been reported pertaining to the area, which include missing planes, missing sea vessels, strange sightings and unexplained magnetic anomalies.

Bicorn: A two horned mythical creature said to grow fat on the flesh of devoted husbands. The configurations of its horns is unknown because it is said to drop them when captured much in the same way some reptiles can drop their tail to escape a predator. Its counterpart is the Chichevache.

Bigfoot: A bulky, hair covered, bipedal humanoid which appears to possess both human and ape-like characteristics. In different regions they are called Sasquatch or Yeti.

Black Magic: Commonly referred to as dark magic, is believed to draw is its power from malevolent sources and is used for evil and/or selfishness purposes.

Black Mass: A perversion of the Christian mass. Black Mass involves various distortions of many Christian rituals aimed at mocking the Christian mass and defiling the communion host.

Bogy: Believed to be an evil spirit or a hobgoblin.

Book of the Dead: An ancient Egyptian collection of hymns, spells and instructions designed to assist the deceased in safe passage in the afterlife. There is speculation that the text is evil in nature.

Book of Thoth: A mystical book containing spells and knowledge, said to have been buried with the Prince Neferkaptah in the City of the Dead. A person who studied from the book would be able to perform amazing feats such as gaining the ability to speak to animals, conjure powerful spells and enchant the earth and the sky. It is said that any human reading from book would be punished by the gods until the book was returned. Also refers to a book by Aleister Crowley that details the use of the tarot card deck.

Botanomancy: A method of divination using burning herbs, tree branches and leaves.

Brontoscopy: A method of divination by listening to the sound of thunder.

Cacodemon: Is an evil spirit or demon.

Cambion: Half-human offspring of either a male human and a succubus or a female human and an incubus. The cambion, upon birth, has no pulse or breath. It's animated but does no exhibit the traditional signs of life. When it reaches about seven years of age it starts to become more difficult to differentiate between it and a normal human. They are usually incredibly beautiful and clever but have evil tendencies due to them being part demon.

Capnomancy: A method of divination by interpreting patterns of smoke.

Cartomancy: Any method of divination using playing cards. Reading tarot cards is a form of cartomancy.

Cerberus: In Greek mythology, a three-headed dog that guards the gates to Hades. His primary purpose is to prevent those who have crossed the river Styx and entered Hades from ever escaping.

Ceroscopy: A method of divination using melted wax poured into cold water. The congealed shapes are interpreted by the diviner.

Champ: Common name for the cryptozoological Monster of Lake Champlain. Similar in description to the Loch Ness monster.

Channeling: The process of communicating with non-physical beings such as spirits.

Charm: This can either refer to a magical spell or incantation or an object that is enchanted with magic such as an amulet or talisman.

Chichevache: A mythical European female monster believed to feed on good and virtuous women. It is said to appear as a cow with a human face.

Chiromancy: A form of Palmistry in which aspects of the palm are read and interpreted to indicate the future outcome and major events that will affect the person whose palm is being read.

Chupacabra: A creature of legend said to inhabit areas of North and South America. It allegedly attacks livestock sucking them dry of their blood. While physical descriptions vary it is believed to be a strong creature about the size of a small bear with a row of spines running from its neck down to the base of its tail.

Clairaudience: Similar to clairvoyance, but specifically related to sounds. Refers to the ability to hear voices and sounds from the paranormal realm.

Clairvoyance: Clairvoyance is a generalized term in the paranormal research world that refers to the ability to gain information about a person, place or object using means other than the normal five senses. It is often what is referred to as a "sixth sense" or Extra Sensory Perception (ESP). It is not the same as telepathy. Telepathy involves, essentially, reading an individual's thoughts and understanding things from their perspective. Clairvoyance is the process of perceiving, beyond ordinary perception, direct and actual information about a person, place or thing.

Cleidomancy: Any method of divination using a key, traditionally suspended as a pendulum.

Cleromancy: Any method of divination done by casting dice, bones, stones or anything that could produce a random outcome. It's believed that the outcome is not truly random but instead can be influenced by God or other supernatural entities.

Close Encounters: A system of classifying UFO sightings, originally suggested by ufologist Josef Allen Hynek in 1972.

Clurichaun: In Irish folklore, a fairy very similar to a leprechaun. Some consider them just a different regional interpretation of the leprechaun.

Cockatrice: A mythical creature with bird wings, a reptilian body, a dragon's tail and a rooster's head. Said to be able to kill with a glance.

Cocytus: Classical name of one of the five rivers encircling Hades in Greek Mythology.

Cold Reading: A technique commonly used in sessions such as psychic readings, in which the person conducting the session elicits information from the subject without their awareness. This is done by skilled reading of body language, age, gender, religion, etc. This information is then used to create the illusion of fortune telling.

Conjuration: The practice of invoking spirits or other non-physical entities by means of ritual activities.

Crop Circles: Any number of large patterns created by flattening crops to form said pattern. These patterns supposedly happen with no known cause although extraterrestrials are suspected.

Crowley, Aleister (Edward Alexander): Aleister Crowley, born Edward Alexander Crowley in Warwickshire England on October 12, 1875. He was brought up in a family very strict with religion. His parents were Exclusive Brethren (a more strict subset of the Plymouth Brethren evangelical Christian group). With the death of his father, Edward, on March 5, 1887 Crowley began to fall away from his religion. His mother's attempts to get him to keep his faith only proved to cause him to migrate further from it. She regularly referred to him as "The Beast", a reference to Satan from the Book of Revelations, in her frustration of his straying from their faith. This is a term Crowley would later adopt fondly. He died December 1, 1947.

Cryokinesis: It is a form of Psychokinesis that refers to the ability to slow atomic motion to the point where a piece of matter freezes. In general it is the ability to remove kinetic energy from a piece of matter. Much like pyrokinesis this ability seems to be more rooted in fiction stories and comic books than actual witnessed psychic phenomena.

Cryptid: Any species of animal which has not been formally identified or categorized by science, e.g. the Yeti.

Cryptozoology: The study and search for those animals whose present-day existence is not formally recognized by mainstream science.

Demon: The word demon, from a Christian perspective, typically is used to label a fallen angel. Angels that, through an opposition to God's law, have fallen away from Him. As a result of their falling away from God, their purposes and interactions are considered evil and contrary to the goodness of God. It should be noted that while modern definition of the word demon relates to evil spirits or fallen angels, in classical Greek writings (from which the word originates) the term simply meant some form of divinity or supernatural being, without the evil connotation associated with it.

Digital Voice Recorder: Is a battery operated device used in everyday life to make audio recordings of sounds. Such devices are used for dictation, note taking or recording lectures. The Digital Voice Recorder is similar to a tape recorder without the tape. The audio signals are stored on internal memory within the recorder for playback at a later time. One of the benefits of using a digital voice recorder over an analog recorder is the reduction of hiss that you would get with an analog based recorder. The digital recorder provides a clearer recording. The purpose of using a voice recorder during a paranormal investigation is the possibility of capturing a disembodied voice, or EVP, during the investigation. EVP stands for Electronic Voice Phenomena and is believed to be the voice of a spirit or entity that is neither visible to the human eye nor able to be heard by unassisted means. This tool should be considered a must have during your paranormal investigations.

Elementals: Mythological beings, originally of alchemy origin, that have a foundation in the core elements of Earth, Air, Fire and Water. Many folklore creatures are affiliated with a specific element and are therefore considered elementals.

EMF Meter: Is a scientific instrument for measuring electromagnetic fields. EMF is an abbreviation for electromagnetic field or electromagnetic fluctuation. Most meters measure the electromagnetic radiation flux density (DC fields) or the change in an electromagnetic field over time (AC fields). The readings are displayed in either Milligauss or Tesla. See also **Mel Meter or K-II**

Enochian: Is a name often applied to an occult or angelic language recorded in the private journals of Dr. John Dee and his seer Edward Kelley in the late 16th century. This language was used in the rituals of both the "Hermetic Order of the Golden Dawn" in the 19th century and the "First Church of Satan" in the 20th century. Some contemporary scholars of magick consider it a constructed language.

Entity: In paranormal terms, a disembodied consciousness capable of interacting with its environment.

EVP: 'Electronic Voice Phenomena.' Disembodied "voices" and sounds imprinted on audio recording devices. These recordings fall into one of three classifications established by Sara Estep who also founded the American Association of Electronic Voice Phenomena:

> **Class A** – A voice or sound that is clearly heard and understood by anyone who listens to it. These EVPs are not processed in any way.
>
> **Class B** – A voice or sound that is heard but may require the assistance of headphones or a noise or hiss reduction process for others to hear. This type of EVP is most common.
>
> **Class C** – A voice or sound that is barley heard. Often these EVPs are faint or a whisper and sometimes indecipherable. They almost always require the assistance of headphones and noise or hiss reduction processing for others to hear.

Extraterrestrials: Describes any life forms that did not originate on Earth.

Ghost: Believed to be a disembodied human soul occupying an area and interacting with objects and people in that area. In can include, but is not limited to, human spirits that sometimes physically manifest themselves in the form of apparitions.

Golden-rod: A rare light anomaly sometimes seen in video footage taken at the site of a suspected haunting. It appears as bright yellow, golden or white lines of light moving across an area.

Grey: This is a term that refers to the most common description of aliens that people have allegedly encountered. The grey typically stands between three and four foot tall, has smooth grey skin with a large oval head. They are hairless and have large, black slanted eyes.

Haunting: The manifestation of paranormal activity, typically associated with the spirit of a decease human. Spiritual haunting can take on one of two forms, active and passive.

Hellhound: A hellhound is a dog of hell. Its origins are found in various mythologies, folklores, and supernatural encounters. They are most frequently described as a large black dog with glowing red or fiery eyes. Typically they are assumed to be strong and threatening. They are often attributed with supernatural properties like the ability to manifest physically and vanish at will. Sometimes they are described as shadow or smoke-like in appearance. In almost all cases their purpose seems to be to guard areas or block passage to certain areas such as cemeteries or burial grounds.

Hex: A magic spell or complex symbol meant to influence another person's will. Typically a hex is a considered to be a negative form of magic, much like a curse.

Homunculus: Any miniaturized from of the human body in which the body is completely formed.

Incubus: (plural incubi): A type of demon, in folklore and legend, that takes on the form of a man. They seduce or force sexual intercourse on humans, especially women. These relations are said to eventually cause failing health and even death. In certain beliefs the incubus, using semen acquired from a man by a succubus, can impregnate a woman.

Infestation: A repeated or persistent paranormal occurrence centered around a specific person or place. It can also refer to a mass occurrence paranormal activity of varying nature focused on a person or place.

Infrared Camera: An infrared Camera is nothing more than a digital or film based camera which has had the infrared filter removed and sometimes replaced with a filter that is designed to block all visible light. The main advantage of an infrared camera is you can photograph objects in total darkness as long as you have an infrared light source.

Jersey Devil: a mythical and folklore creature said to live in the Pine Barrens region of New Jersey. The origins of the story date back to the 1800's as do the sightings of the cryptid. The creature itself is most often describes as being bipedal with hooves. It has a horse-like head and bat-like wings.

K-II Meter: The K-II meter is a scientific instrument used for measuring electromagnetic fields. This meter has been used by paranormal investigators to attempt to communicate with spirits encountered on investigations due to the fact that the LED lights are easy to read. This is a only theory due to the lack of evidence supporting communication.

Kirlian Photography: A type of photography that involves a object on a photographic plate being exposed to high voltage. The result is an image that shows a corona discharge created by the electric field. This concept was named after Semyon Kirlian who in 1939 invented this process. He went on to suggest that the energy viewed around the edge of an object may be similar to that of the human aura. It gained popularity, although not among the scientific community, as a way to photograph aura energy.

Loch Ness Monster: The Loch Ness Monster is a creature that is alleged to live in the depths of Loch Ness in the Scottish Highlands. Stories of lake and river monsters in this area of Scotland have existed since the 6th century A.D. Recent interest in the idea of a monster in Loch Ness started with a single eye witness account in 1933. The creature, as reported by those who claimed to have seen it through the decades, describe some common features. The creature is described as dark gray or blackish in color. It is around 20-25 feet long. Its skin is described as thick and elephant like. It has a reasonably slender body with a long neck and small head. It has also been described with small forelegs or flippers. Similar flippers may be present in the form of hind appendages as well. The most descriptive accounts come from alleged encounters with the creature out of the water as it moved along the shoreline or across roads.

Lycanthrope: A person who is capable of shaft-shifting from man to wolf and back to man. *See Werewolf.*

Magic: A broad category describing the practice of invoking energies, spirits, elementals or other entities by use of spells and incantations to do the will of the practitioner of magic.

Mel Meter: The Mel Meter Model 8704 is an intelligent microprocessor based instrument specifically designed for Paranormal Investigators & Enthusiasts. Several Important features have been incorporated into this durable, precision hand held instrument, all of them accessible with the meter being held in one hand. The Mel Meter is the only meter that can measure EMF and temperature "Cold Spots" at the same time. It has been the generally accepted theory that spirits do emit an extremely low frequency (ULF / ELF) EM field, which commonly registers between 2.0 and 7.0 mG in strength. Typically, anything below 40Hz would be considered part of the ELF range. The Mel-8704-2X was designed to address the ULF & ELF range simultaneously.

Necronomicon: A collection of ancient symbols, incantations and religious concepts identifying god-like entities possibly dating back to ancient Sumeria. Supposedly discovered in the 8th century by the "Mad Arab," Abdul Alhazred. There is strong believe that then the Necronomicon was a complete fabrication of H.P. Lovecraft.

Necromancy: The practice of communicating with the dead, either as an apparition or spirit, or to reanimate their body for the purpose of divination.

Nemesis: Greek mythology's goddess of justice and vengeance.

Ogopogo: Similar to the Loch Ness Monster, Ogopogo is the name given to a creature that allegedly lives in Okanagan Lake in Canada. The first documented sightings of the creature date back to the late 1800's. Most sightings of the creature in which details about it were clear and visible have no evidence, outside of witness testimony, to back them up. Most video or photographic evidence, although often unclear and difficult to make out, seems to coincide with the personal accounts and paints a picture of a large serpentine creature. Some claim the few photos and video evidence coupled with the personal accounts indicate the creature could be an animal similar to a Basilosaurus which is a primitive form of whale that lived 34 to 40 million years ago in the Late Eocene period.

Orb: A common anomaly caught on photographic or video footage taken at the site of suspected paranormal activity. They appear as small white, semi-transparent balls or orbs. Most often dust or insects are mistakenly identified as these anomalies. It's believed by some that the presences of these globules, or orbs, are an indication of paranormal energy or a spiritual presence.

Ouija (Board): A device consisting of a board with letters, numbers, words, and sometimes symbols. Some sort of pointing device, often called a planchette, is also used. The people using the board place their hands on the planchette and ask the spirits questions. It is believed that the spirits can manipulate the movements of the planchette and spell out messages. Original designed as a parlor game it gained popularity in the occult and paranormal studies when American spiritualist Pearl Curran used it as a diving tool in World War I.

Paranormal: General term referring to the realm of things outside of normal or scientific explanation. Often used interchangeably with supernatural. It literally can be translated to "beyond normal".

Parapsychology: Considered a pseudoscience aimed at studying paranormal and supernatural concepts such as hauntings, psychics, near death experiences, etc.

Paraeidolia: Psychological phenomenon in which something random appears to be of significance. It's the natural tendency of the human brain to attempt to translate things into something useful. Seeing the face of the "man on the moon" or seeing animals in the clouds are example.

Passive Haunt: Activity witnessed that is nothing more than an event from the past being played over and over again. This theory suggests that energy emitted from the living at times of great stress or trauma can be absorbed and stored by inanimate objects and then played back over and over during the right conditions, producing a scene from the past. The activity witnessed does not interact with the living and show no signs of acknowledgment to those who witness it.

Precognition: Precognition literally mean to "know before" or to "know prior to". It refers to the ability to predict future events. These predictions or perceptions of events that will occur in the future are derived by means other than the known facts of the moment.

Psychic: A person claiming to perceive information from means other than the five natural senses. Someone skilled in utilizing various forms of extra sensory perception (ESP).

Psychokinesis: Psychokinesis, also known as Telekinesis, refers to the ability to manipulate matter and energy without making physical contact. It typically refers to the ability of a person to use his/her mind to control and manipulate objects in a physical way, although it can also refer to the ability to influence things such as an electronic random number generator or other electronic device. It is also used as a global or umbrella term to represent a number of other psychic abilities that fall under the general concept of manipulating the environment with one's mind. It is often abbreviated as PK for Psychokinesis or TK for Telekinesis.

Pyrokinesis: It is a form of psychokinesis that refers to the ability to excite the atoms in a piece of matter to the point of combustion. A number of experts in the paranormal field do not recognize pyrokinesis as an actual paranormal ability. It is generally believed to simply be a production of fictional stories, such as Stephen King's Firestarter, and comic books.

Spirit: The life force of an organism. The non-physical part of an Entity's existence. The term is often used interchangeably with the term ghost and references to the lingering soul of a deceased human.

Spook: Another term for a ghost, spirit or apparition.

Succubus: (plural succubi) A type of demon, in folklore and legend, which takes the form of a woman in order to seduce men. They seduce or force men, either in a waking state or in dreams, to have sexual intercourse with them. They draw energy from their victims by this process and exhaust and potentially kill their victims over time. In more modern lore the succubi are depicted as attractive. Traditionally they were depicted as ugly.

There are other beliefs the succubi not only draw energy from their victims but actually collect semen as well which they hand off to their male counterparts, the incubi. The incubi then use this semen to impregnate women. This was sometimes used to explain deformed children or children that appeared to be more tuned into the supernatural world.

Tape Recorder: Is a battery operated device used in everyday life to make audio recordings of sounds. Such devices are used for dictation, note taking or recording lectures. The Tape Recorder is used to record audio signals which are stored on magnetic tape for playback at a later time. The Tape Recorder is also referred to as an analog recorder and is known to produce a hiss if an external microphone is not used during the recording process. The purpose of using a tape recorder during a paranormal investigation is the possibility of capturing a disembodied voice, or EVP, during the investigation. See also **EVP**

Telekinesis: *See Psychokinesis*

Telepathy: Telepathy, from the Greek language tele meaning distant, and patheia meaning feeling, centers around the idea of an individual being able to sense or read thoughts and emotions of another individual using means other than the traditional five sense of touch, smell, sight, hearing and taste. This concept covers both the ability to read another persons thoughts and emotions as well as pushing thoughts and emotions to other individuals. There is little evidence of telepathy in historic records. It is generally believed that the concept of telepathy came into being in the western scientific world in the late 1800's and early 1900's with the study of "thought transference". Research by the Society for Psychical Research gave birth to the term telepathy.

Most of the study of this work by the Society for Psychical Research and other researchers of that time, was done by researching personal accounts and performing some basic experiments.

Thermal Imaging Camera: A thermal imaging camera is a type of thermo graphic camera used to render infrared radiation as visible light. Such cameras allow the user to see areas of heat through smoke, darkness, or heat-permeable barriers. Thermal imaging cameras are typically handheld, constructed using heat and water-resistant housings, and are ruggedized. While they are expensive pieces of equipment, they are highly coveted by Paranormal Investigators.

Therianthropy: Therianthropy is the general category of shape shifting in which man or woman is able to transform into animal and back. It is the super category of all human to animal shape shifters. The most well known of the type of therianthropy is lycanthropy (human-wolf transformation). Therianthropy has permeated cultures, mythologies, and lore for millennia.

Thought Transference: A form of telepathy involved the transmission of thoughts from the mind of one person to another.

TriField Natural EM Meter: The TriField Natural EM Meter was designed to do field measurements for special research. It detects changes in extremely weak static (DC or "natural") electric and magnetic fields, and signals with both a tone and the movement of a needle-type gauge if either the electric or magnetic field changes from previous levels. A radio and microwave detector is also included which reads radio power directly. Because man-made AC electric and magnetic fields are very common and could interfere with readings of static fields, the meter has been designed to ignore AC fields. Normal construction materials don't block magnetic fields, so the meter can be placed indoors and will work equally well. Due to the built-in tone, it can be used in the dark and will sound the tone at whatever level of field the user sets. Model 1 operates on a standard 9-volt battery, and Model 2 runs on a 9-volt battery or an AC adapter (both included). Model 2 has an input jack for an optional high-sensitivity magnetic coil.

Ultra-terrestrials: Not to be confused with Extraterrestrials, Ultra-terrestrials are superhuman beings. It is believed that these beings exist on Earth in our three dimensional plane of existence but can travel beyond it. The Greek and roman gods and goddesses, faeries, and other such beings fit into this classification.

Vampire: Folklore beings that subsist by feeding on the life essence of living creatures. This is often assumed to be blood but does not necessarily have to be. Although history evolved the vampire into a creature that is essentially the reanimated dead, traditionally vampires can be living beings or the undead.

Voodoo: A system of religious with African traditions at its core but heavily infused with Catholic concepts. The beliefs associated with Voodoo vary from person to person but in general there is believed to be one God who does not interfere with humans on a day to day basis. Spirits however can and do interfere with humans regularly. Connection with these spirits is achieved through dance, singing and other rituals.

Warlock: A term certain cultures use to refer to a male witch.

Werewolf: A human being capable of shape shifting from human to wolf and back to human again. In some translations having this ability is seen as the result of an animal bite and treated almost as a disease. In other translation it's viewed as a power that can be controlled by the individual.

Wicca: A religion based primary on the forces of nature. Although there is variety within the overall practice as to the details of the aspect of worship, in general there are universally two deities that are worshiped. One is a male god, usually representing nature, wilderness, sexuality, hunting and the life cycle and the other is a female goddess representing namely virginity, fertility and wisdom.

Witch: A practitioner of the magic arts, either man or woman who uses natural magic to do his/her will. Historically both good and bad witched have been believed to exist. Also, a male or female who practices Wicca.

Xenobiology: It is a field of biology that focuses on the possible of alien and artificial life.

Xenophobia: A deep-rooted fear and hatred of strangers or anything that is foreign or strange.

Yeti: A legendary creature said to inhabit the Himalayan Mountain region. Very similar to its western counterpart, Bigfoot, it is a large humanoid creature that appears to be a mix of human and ape. It is also known as the Abominable Snow Man.

Zombie: A reanimated human corpse or an entranced living person being controlled by magical means. Typically zombies are Voodoo related.

Bibliography

Bauer, H. (1992). Scientific Literacy and the Myth of the Scientific Method
University of Illinois Press

Bernstein, R. (1983). Beyond Objectivism and Relativism: Science, Hermeneutics, and Praxis
University of Pennsylvania Press

Eoghan, C. (2010). Digital Evidence and Computer Crime
Academic Press

Estep, S. (1988). Voices of Eternity
Ballantine Books.

Franklin, J. (2009), What Science Knows: And How it Knows it
Encounter Books

Heinemanm, K. (2007). The Orb Project
Beyond Words Publishing

Heuvelmans, B. (1996). On the Track of Unknown Animals
Columbia University Press.

Lewis, S. (1964). The Discarded Image: An Introduction to Medieval and Renaissance Literature
Cambridge University Press.

Matthews, J. (2006). The Element Encyclopedia of Magical Creatures: The Ultimate A-Z of Fantastic Beings From Myth and Magic
Sterling Publishing.

Newton, (1999). Rules for the study of natural philosophy
The System of the World.

Shermer, M. (2003). Show Me the Body
Scientific America

Wentizenhoffer, A. (1980), Hypnotic Susceptibility Revisited
American Journal of Clinical Hypnosis

Wilson, C. (2008). The Mammoth Encyclopedia of the Unsolved
Unlimited Press.

"C7-P3- 78,
C2-P18-128,
C4-P6-12 C2-P13-24 C7-P1-64 C9-P1-84"

The Supernatural Research Group
www.tsrg.org

www.ingramcontent.com/pod-product-compliance
Lightning Source LLC
Chambersburg PA
CBHW030934090426
42737CB00007B/431